31

STUDY GUIDE

The First World War, 1914 - 1918

CIE

app available

Published by Clever Lili Limited.

contact@cleverlili.com

First published 2020

ISBN 978-1-913887-30-8

Cover by: Lieutenant Ernest Brookes on Wikimedia Commons

Icons by: flaticon and freepik

Contributors: Jonathan Boyd, James George, Marcus Pailing, Jen Mellors

Edited by Paul Connolly and Rebecca Parsley

Design by Evgeni Veskov and Will Fox

DISCOVER MORE OF OUR IGCSE HISTORY STUDY GUIDES

GCSEHistory.com and Clever Lili

CIE

STUDY GUIDE

**International Relations:
Were the Peace Treaties of 1919-23 Fair?**

GCSEHistory.com

17

CIE

STUDY GUIDE

**International Relations:
To What Extent Was the League of
Nations a Success?**

GCSEHistory.com

18

CIE

STUDY GUIDE

**International Relations:
Why Had International Peace Collapsed
by 1939?**

GCSEHistory.com

19

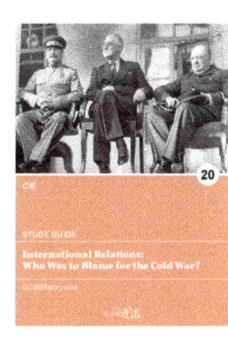

CIE

STUDY GUIDE

**International Relations:
Who Was to Blame for the Cold War?**

GCSEHistory.com

20

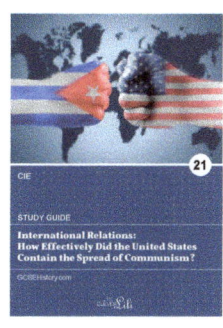

CIE

STUDY GUIDE

**International Relations:
How Effectively Did the United States
Contain the Spread of Communism?**

GCSEHistory.com

21

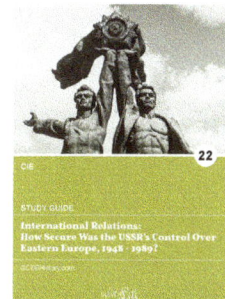

CIE

STUDY GUIDE

**International Relations:
How Secure Was the USSR's Control Over
Eastern Europe, 1948 - 1989?**

GCSEHistory.com

22

CIE

STUDY GUIDE

**International Relations:
Why Did Events in the Gulf Matter
c1970 - 2000?**

GCSEHistory.com

23

CIE

STUDY GUIDE

The United States, 1919 - 1941

GCSEHistory.com

32

CIE

STUDY GUIDE

Russia, 1905 - 1941

GCSEHistory.com

33

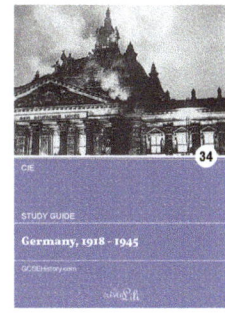

CIE

STUDY GUIDE

Germany, 1918 - 1945

GCSEHistory.com

34

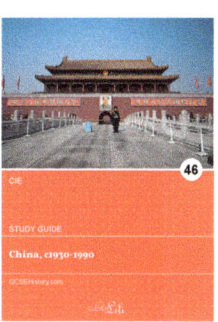

CIE

STUDY GUIDE

China, c1930-1990

GCSEHistory.com

46

THE GUIDES ARE EVEN BETTER WITH OUR GCSE/IGCSE HISTORY WEBSITE APP AND MOBILE APP

GCSE History is a text and voice web and mobile app that allows you to easily revise for your GCSE/IGCSE exams wherever you are - it's like having your own personal GCSE history tutor. Whether you're at home or on the bus, GCSE History provides you with thousands of convenient bite-sized facts to help you pass your exams with flying colours. We cover all topics - with more than 120,000 questions - across the Edexcel, AQA and CIE exam boards.

GCSEHistory.com

GET IT ON
Google Play

Download on the
App Store

Contents

In this study guide, you will see a series of icons, highlighted words and page references. The key below will help you quickly establish what these mean and where to go for more information.

Icons

 WHAT questions cover the key events and themes.

 WHO questions cover the key people involved.

 WHEN questions cover the timings of key events.

 WHERE questions cover the locations of key moments.

 WHY questions cover the reasons behind key events.

 HOW questions take a closer look at the way in which events, situations and trends occur.

 IMPORTANCE questions take a closer look at the significance of events, situations, and recurrent trends and themes.

DECISIONS questions take a closer look at choices made at events and situations during this era.

Highlighted words

Abdicate - occasionally, you will see certain words highlighted within an answer. This means that, if you need it, you'll find an explanation of the word or phrase in the glossary which starts on **page 97**.

Page references

Tudor *(p. 7)* - occasionally, a certain subject within an answer is covered in more depth on a different page. If you'd like to learn more about it, you can go directly to the page indicated.

Quizzes, amazing exam preparation tools and more at GCSEHistory.com

This unit focuses on the course and key events of the First World War, from its outbreak in 1914 until the Armistice was signed in 1918.

Purpose

The purpose of this course is to investigate the nature of fighting and life during the First World War, and to develop an understanding of the course of events during the war, and how they ultimately led to the signing of the Armistice in November 1914.

Topics

This unit gives you the information you need to understand the following:

- The reasons why the war was not over by December 1914, including the failure of the Schlieffen Plan, the extent of the British Expeditionary Force's success and the introduction of the trench system.

- The reasons for the stalemate on the Western Front, including the nature of trench warfare and life in the trenches, the importance of new technological developments and the significance of Verdun and the Somme.

- The importance of other fronts, including the War at Sea, Russia and the Eastern Front, and the home fronts.

- The reasons for Germany's request for an Armistice in 1918, including the USA's 1917 entry into the war, the failure of the Ludendorff Offensive, the German Revolution of 1918, and the reasons for the signing of the Armistice.

Key Individuals

Some of the key individuals studied on this course include:

- Lord Kitchener.
- Field Marshal Foch.
- Field Marshal Haig.
- Admiral Jellicoe.
- Admiral Scheer.
- General Brusilov.
- General Ludendorff.

Key Events

Some of the key events you will study on this course include:

- The Schlieffen Plan in operation.
- The Battles of Mons, the Marne and Ypres.
- The reaction to the stalemate.
- The nature and problems of trench warfare.
- The main battles of the war including Verdun and the Somme.
- The nature of problems of trench warfare.
- The impact of technological advances.
- The Battle of Jutland and its consequences.
- The use of convoys, submarines and the U-boat campaign.
- The reasons for, and results of the Gallipoli campaign.
- The impact of war on civilian populations.
- Events on the Eastern Front and the surrender of Russia.
- The German offensive and Allied advance.
- The impact of American entry into the war.
- Conditions in Germany by the end of the war.
- The Kiel Mutiny and German Revolution.
- The abdication of the Kaiser.
- The Armistice.

Assessment

The First World War is one of the specified depth studies found in Paper 1, where you have a total of 2 hours to complete 3 questions. You must answer 2 questions from the core section of the paper and one question from a choice of two questions on your chosen depth study. Therefore, you will answer one question on the First World War if this is your chosen depth study. The question is comprised of 3 sections; a), b), and c).

- Question a is worth 4 marks. This question will require you to describe key features of the time period. You will be asked to recall 2 relevant points and support them with details or provide at least four relevant points without supporting detail.

- Question b is worth 6 marks. This question will require you to explain a key event or development. You will need to identify two reasons, support those reasons with relevant factual detail and then explain how the reasons made the event occur.

- Question c is worth 10 marks. This question will require you to construct an argument to support and challenge an interpretation stated in the question. You will need to have a minimum of three explanations (two on one side and one on the other) in total, fully evaluate the argument and come to a justified conclusion. You will have the opportunity to show your ability to explain and analyse historical events using 2nd order concepts such as causation, consequence, change, continuity, similarity and difference.

- The First World War may also appear on Paper 4, a one-hour paper in which you will give an extended answer to one question about this topic. Check with your teacher to find out if you will be taking this option.

Revision! A dreaded word. Everyone knows it's coming, everyone knows how much it helps with your exam performance, and everyone struggles to get started! We know you want to do the best you can in your IGCSEs, but schools aren't always clear on the best way to revise. This can leave students wondering:

- ✔ How should I plan my revision time?
- ✔ How can I beat procrastination?
- ✔ What methods should I use? Flash cards? Re-reading my notes? Highlighting?

Luckily, you no longer need to guess at the answers. Education researchers have looked at all the available revision studies, and the jury is in. They've come up with some key pointers on the best ways to revise, as well as some thoughts on popular revision methods that aren't so helpful. The next few pages will help you understand what we know about the best revision methods.

 ## How can I beat procrastination?

This is an age-old question, and it applies to adults as well! Have a look at our top three tips below.

◎ Reward yourself

When we think a task we have to do is going to be boring, hard or uncomfortable, we often put if off and do something more 'fun' instead. But we often don't really enjoy the 'fun' activity because we feel guilty about avoiding what we should be doing. Instead, get your work done and promise yourself a reward after you complete it. Whatever treat you choose will seem all the sweeter, and you'll feel proud for doing something you found difficult. Just do it!

◎ Just do it!

We tend to procrastinate when we think the task we have to do is going to be difficult or dull. The funny thing is, the most uncomfortable part is usually making ourselves sit down and start it in the first place. Once you begin, it's usually not nearly as bad as you anticipated.

◎ Pomodoro technique

The pomodoro technique helps you trick your brain by telling it you only have to focus for a short time. Set a timer for 20 minutes and focus that whole period on your revision. Turn off your phone, clear your desk, and work. At the end of the 20 minutes, you get to take a break for five. Then, do another 20 minutes. You'll usually find your rhythm and it becomes easier to carry on because it's only for a short, defined chunk of time.

 ## Spaced practice

We tend to arrange our revision into big blocks. For example, you might tell yourself: "This week I'll do all my revision for the Cold War, then next week I'll do the Medicine Through Time unit."

This is called **massed practice**, because all revision for a single topic is done as one big mass.

But there's a better way! Try **spaced practice** instead. Instead of putting all revision sessions for one topic into a single block, space them out. See the example below for how it works.

This means planning ahead, rather than leaving revision to the last minute - but the evidence strongly suggests it's worth it. You'll remember much more from your revision if you use **spaced practice** rather than organising it into big blocks. Whichever method you choose, though, remember to reward yourself with breaks.

Spaced practice (more effective):

week 1	week 2	week 3	week 4
Topic 1	Topic 1	Topic 1	Topic 1
Topic 2	Topic 2	Topic 2	Topic 2
Topic 3	Topic 3	Topic 3	Topic 3
Topic 4	Topic 4	Topic 4	Topic 4

Massed practice (less effective)

week 1	week 2	week 3	week 4
Topic 1	Topic 2	Topic 3	Topic 4

What methods should I use to revise?

Self-testing/flash cards	Self explanation/mind-mapping

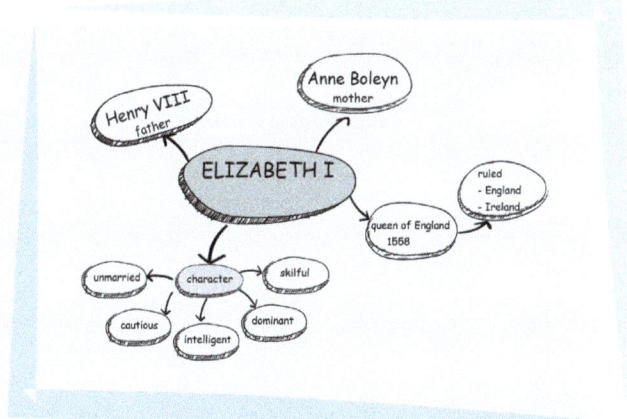

The research shows a clear winner for revision methods - **self-testing**. A good way to do this is with **flash cards**. Flash cards are really useful for helping you recall short – but important – pieces of information, like names and dates.

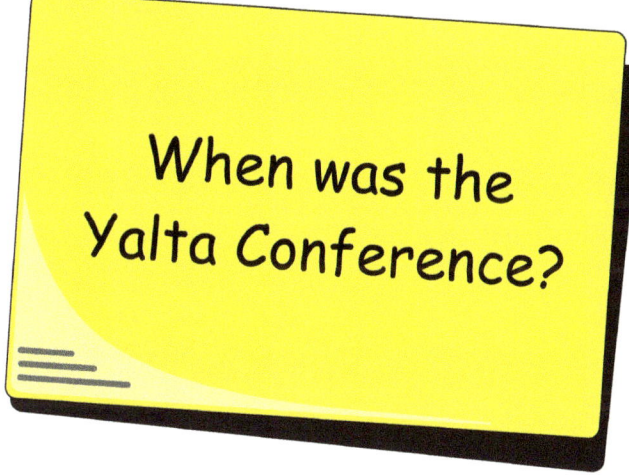

Side A - question

Side B - answer

Write questions on one side of the cards, and the answers on the back. This makes answering the questions and then testing yourself easy. Put all the cards you get right in a pile to one side, and only repeat the test with the ones you got wrong - this will force you to work on your weaker areas.

pile with right answers

pile with wrong answers

As this book has a quiz question structure itself, you can use it for this technique.

Another good revision method is **self-explanation**. This is where you explain how and why one piece of information from your course linked with another piece.

This can be done with **mind-maps**, where you draw the links and then write explanations for how they connect. For example, President Truman is connected with anti-communism because of the Truman Doctrine.

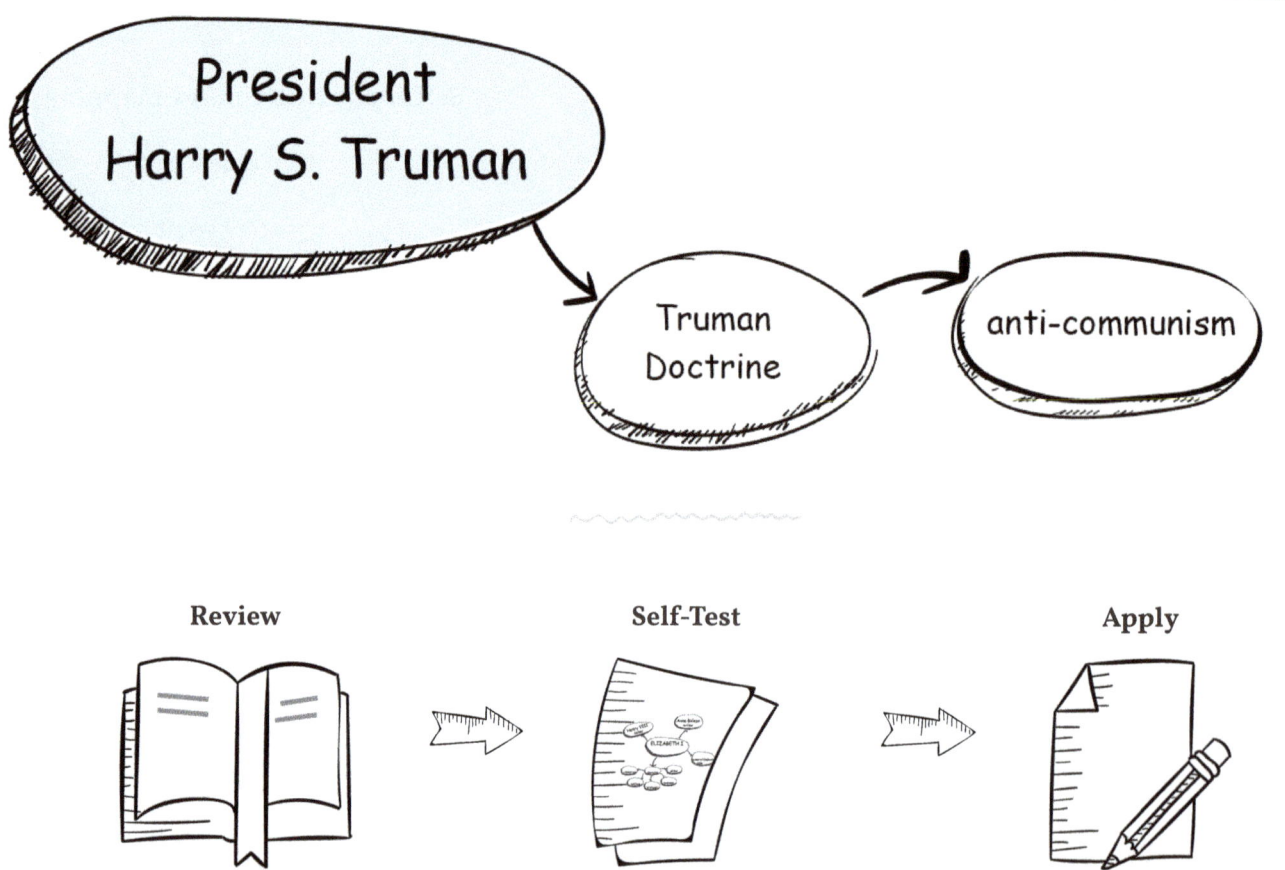

Review

Start by highlighting or re-reading to create your flashcards for self-testing.

Self-Test

Test yourself with flash cards. Make mind maps to explain the concepts.

Apply

Apply your knowledge on practice exam questions.

 ## Which revision techniques should I be cautious about?

Highlighting and **re-reading** are not necessarily bad strategies - but the research does say they're less effective than flash cards and mind-maps.

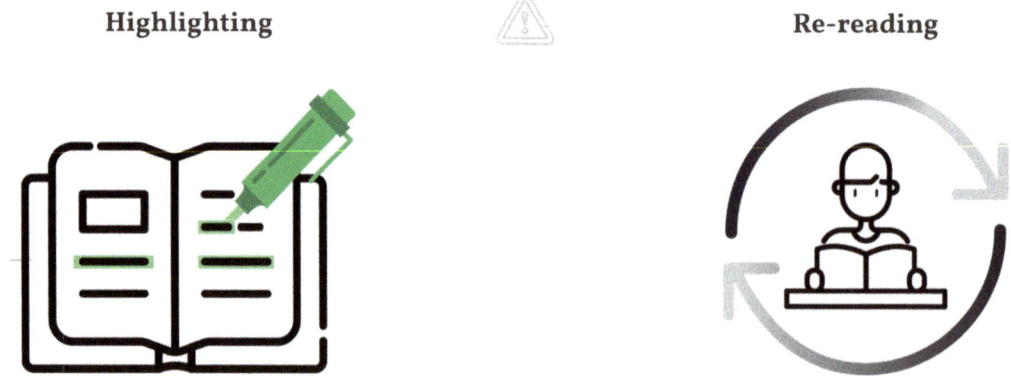

Highlighting

Re-reading

If you do use these methods, make sure they are **the first step to creating flash cards**. Really engage with the material as you go, rather than switching to autopilot.

TIMELINE

1914

28th June - Assassination of Franz Ferdinand *(p.25)*

5th July - Germany offers support to Austria (the 'blank cheque') *(p.26)*

23rd July - Austria sends ultimatum to Serbia *(p.26)*

25th July - Serbia rejects ultimatum *(p.26)*

28th July - Austria declares war on Serbia *(p.26)*

1st August - Germany declares war on Russia *(p.26)*

3rd August - Germany declares war on France *(p.26)*

3rd August - Germany invades Belgium *(p.26)*

4th August - Britain declares war on Germany *(p.26)*

11th August - Defence of the Realm Act introduced in Britain *(p.78)*

September - Battle of the Marne *(p.26)*

Sept - Oct - Race to the sea establishes Western Front

October - Turkey enters the war *(p.52)*

1915

Feb 1915 - Jan 1916 - Gallipoli Campaign *(p.52)*

April - First use of poison gas on the Western Front *(p.40)*

7th May - Sinking of the Lusitania *(p.51)*

December - Haig becomes Commander-in-Chief of the BEF *(p.91)*

1916

Jan - Dec - Battle of Verdun *(p.44)*

31st May - 1st June - Battle of Jutland *(p.49)*

1st July - 21st Nov - Battle of the Somme *(p.45)*

August - Creeping barrage tactic begins to be used *(p.42)*

September - First use of tanks *(p.41)*

Winter 1916-1917 - 'Turnip winter' in Germany

1917

January - Zimmerman Telegram sent *(p.76)*

1st Feb - Germany resumes unrestricted U-boat warfare *(p.49)*

2nd April - USA declares war on Germany *(p.76)*

July - Sept - Battle of Passchendaele *(p.46)*

October - Russian Revolution *(p.71)*

November - Successful massed tank attack at Battle of Cambrai *(p.41)*

1918

March - Foch becomes Commander-in-Chief of all Allied forces on the Western Front *(p.91)*

March - Russia signs peace treaty with Germany *(p.71)*

March - July - Ludendorff Offensive *(p.84)*

8th Aug - 11th Nov - Allied 100 Days Offensive *(p.85)*

October - German navy mutinies

9th Nov - Kaiser Wilhelm II abdicates *(p.89)*

11th Nov - Armistice signed *(p.89)*

THE GREAT POWERS

The most powerful countries.

 What were the Great Powers?

The Great Powers were the most powerful countries in Europe in the years before the First World War *(p. 23)*. Their competing foreign policies increased tensions between them which ultimately led to the outbreak of war in 1914.

 Who were the Great Powers?

There were 5 Great Powers in 1914:

- ☑ Great Britain.
- ☑ Germany.
- ☑ France.
- ☑ Austria-Hungary.
- ☑ Russia.

 What were the characteristics of a Great Power?

To be a great power in 1914 a country had to meet the following criteria:

- ☑ Be able to influence and control international affairs.
- ☑ Possess great economic strength.
- ☑ Possess great military power.
- ☑ Possess a stable and competent government.
- ☑ Rule over a large population of people.
- ☑ Control a large empire that possesses lots of resources.

 Which countries were not considered Great Powers but were considered second-rate powers?

There were 4 second-rate powers in 1914:

- ☑ Italy.
- ☑ The Ottoman Empire.
- ☑ Japan.
- ☑ The USA.

DID YOU KNOW?

The First World War was what we call a 'total war' because the entire population and all of the resources of each nation had to be used to try and win the military struggle.

BRITAIN

The British bulldog.

 ## What was Britain like in 1914?

In 1914 Britain was the wealthiest country in the world. However, its dominance was under threat from other industrialising countries.

 ## What was British foreign policy in 1914?

Britain's foreign policy had experienced significant change by 1914 *(p.23)*:

- ☑ In the late nineteenth century, Britain had avoided getting involved in European affairs through its policy of 'splendid isolation'.
- ☑ In the early 1900s, Britain abandoned this 'splendid isolation' due to the growing threat from Germany.
- ☑ Britain became part of the Triple Entente *(p.24)* by 1907.
- ☑ Imperialism was strong in Britain. It possessed the world's most powerful *(p.16)* navy and largest merchant fleet.
- ☑ Britain wanted a balance of power *(p.16)* in Europe and always put the defence of the empire first.

 ## What was the British economy like in 1914?

By the start of the twentieth century, Britain was the wealthiest country in the world.

- ☑ London was the centre of global finance.
- ☑ Much of this wealth came from the empire, which was the largest in the world in 1914.
- ☑ However, the economy was in decline as Germany and the USA were overtaking Britain in areas such as coal and iron production.

 ## What was the British government like in 1914?

Britain a constitutional monarchy whose head of state was King George V.

 ## What was the population of Britain in 1914?

Britain ruled over 41 million citizens internally and another 390 million subjects in its colonies.

DID YOU KNOW?

Another character that is often used to represent the British 'bulldog' spirit is 'John Bull'. He was portrayed as a plump, wealthy farmer wearing a union flag waistcoat.

FRANCE

The French cockerel.

What was France like in 1914?

France was economically strong in 1914 and had the second-largest empire in the world, with many trade links.

What was the foreign policy of France in 1914?

Much of French foreign policy centred on the threat from Germany:

- ✅ France wanted revenge on Germany for her defeat in the Franco-Prussian war of 1870, and to regain the rich provinces of Alsace and Lorraine that had been lost after the war.
- ✅ France, therefore, signed military alliances with Russia and Britain to protect herself from German attack.
- ✅ Militarism was important in France as she underwent large scale rearmament before 1914 to rival Germany.

 What was the French economy like in 1914?

France was an industrialised nation by 1914 (p.23):

- ✅ It had well developed industries.
- ✅ It was a leader in science and technology.
- ✅ It possessed a large agricultural sector.

 What was the French empire like 1914?

France's empire played an important role in its economy:

- ✅ It had the second largest empire in the world after Britain.
- ✅ It was a strong trading nation.
- ✅ Much of its wealth came from its Asian and African colonies but despite this the economy was weaker than Germany's.

 What was the French government like in 1914?

France was a republic with an elected head of state and an elected prime minister.

 What was the population of France in 1914?

France ruled over 40 million citizens internally and another 58 million subjects in its empire.

DID YOU KNOW?

An alternative character associated with the spirit of the French Republic is the revolutionary character 'Marianne'. She was portrayed as a beautiful woman, sometimes wearing a red cap.

RUSSIA

The Russian bear.

 What was Russia like in 1914?

Russia was the largest Great Power (p.16), but also the most backward. Its economy was mainly agricultural and its armed forces were poorly equipped.

 What was Russia's foreign policy in 1914?

Russia had 2 main foreign policies in 1914.

- ✅ It feared the growing strength (p.16) of Germany, so made alliances with France and Britain.

☑ As fellow Slavs, Russia supported the Serbs in their struggle against Austria-Hungary in the Balkans.

What was the Russian economy like in 1914?

The Russian economy was mainly agricultural and its industrial base was small compared to other great powers.

What was the military like in Russia 1914?

The Russian military was large but not advanced. It was poorly equipped and made up of conscripted peasants, who made poor soldiers.

How strong was nationalism in Russia in 1914?

Nationalism was very strong in Russia in 1914.

What was Russia's influence in the Balkans in 1914?

Russia had suffered an embarrassing defeat against Japan in 1905, which weakened Russian influence in the Balkans.

What was the population of Russia in 1914?

Russia's population was more than 170 million, few of which had rights or protections. There was growing discontent throughout the empire.

Who was the leader of Russia in 1914?

Tsar Nicholas II was an autocrat who was unsuited to ruling such a corrupt and problematic empire.

DID YOU KNOW?

A different symbol for Russia from the tsarist period was the double headed eagle taken from the coat of arms of the Romanov family.

GERMANY

The German eagle.

What was Germany like in 1914?

By 1914 *(p.23)* Germany had the second biggest industrial capacity in the world (after the USA). It had a small empire compared to the other Great Powers.

What was German foreign policy in 1914?

There were 3 main aspects to German foreign policy before 1914 *(p.23)*:

☑ Germany feared encirclement by Russia and France so formed the Triple Alliance *(p.24)* in 1882 and increased the size of its army.

☑ Kaiser Wilhelm II believed that Germany should have its 'place in the sun' - a large overseas empire befitting its Great Power *(p.16)* status. This was called weltpolitik (world policy) and required the building of a large navy.

☑ Formed in 1871, Germany upset the balance of power *(p.16)* in Europe by defeating France in the Franco-Prussian War of 1870-71 and creating a rivalry with Russia and Britain.

What was German industry like in 1914?

By 1914 *(p.23)*, Germany had the second biggest industrial capacity in the world (after the USA).

 Who was the leader of Germany in 1914?

The German head of state was a kaiser (emperor). From 1888 this was Kaiser Wilhelm II. He was:

- ☑ An erratic ruler, impulsive and prone to outbursts of rage.
- ☑ An autocrat. Although he was meant to rule alongside his appointed government he often ignored advice from his government ministers.
- ☑ A cousin of King George V and Tsar Nicholas II.
- ☑ Plagued by feelings of inadequacy when Germany was matched against larger empires. This contributed to his decision to go to war in 1914.

 What was the German empire like in 1914?

Germany had a small empire compared to the other Great Powers. However, the kaiser had pursued an empire-building policy, which had brought Germany into conflict with Britain and France.

 What was the German military like in 1914?

Germany was a powerful *(p.16)* military nation by 1914 *(p.23)*.

- ☑ Militarism and imperialism were important in Germany.
- ☑ The powerful *(p.16)* economy enabled Germany to build the largest and most modern army in Europe.
- ☑ Germany challenged Britain for control *(p.16)* of the seas.

 What was the German government like in 1914?

Germany had an elected parliament and political parties, but the government and all its policies were controlled by the autocratic kaiser. This created great political tension in Germany before 1914.

 What was the German population in 1914?

Germany ruled over 65 million citizens internally and another 15 million people in its empire.

DID YOU KNOW?

Wilhelm II of Germany was a first cousin to Tsar Nicholas II of Russia and King George V of Great Britain. The three cousins were all related to each other through Queen Victoria.

AUSTRIA-HUNGARY

The Austrian black eagle.

 What was Austria like in 1914?

Austria-Hungary was the weakest of the Great Powers after Russia, with a large but poorly equipped army.

What was the Austro-Hungarian Empire like before 1914?

Austria-Hungary had a European empire containing many ethnic groups and languages, many of whom wanted independence.

What affected Austro-Hungarian foreign policy before 1914?

There were 2 main influences on Austria-Hungary's foreign policy:

- ☑ Domestic nationalism and racism were powerful *(p.16)* forces in Austria-Hungary that created constant tensions with Serbia and Russia over the Balkans.
- ☑ The rise of a newly independent Serbia, supported by Russia, was considered a great threat to the integrity of the Austrian-Hungarian Empire.

What was the foreign policy of Austria before the First World War?

Austria-Hungarian foreign policy had 3 main aims:

- ☑ To limit the power *(p.16)* of the newly independent Serbia because it was encouraging the Slavic people of the empire to push for independence.
- ☑ To keep its fragmenting empire together.
- ☑ To increase its influence in the Balkans and therefore, limit Serbian and Russian influence in the region.

What was the Austrian government like in 1914?

The main features of the Austro-Hungarian government were:

- ☑ An autocratic emperor as head of state, with overall control *(p.16)* of both states. From 1848 this was Franz Josef I.
- ☑ Two parliaments (one each for Austria and Hungary) that governed their respective parts of the empire.

What was the Emperor of the Austrian government like in 1914?

Franz Josef I was out of touch with the modern world, and obsessed with reasserting Austrian power *(p.16)* in the Balkans at all costs.

What was the Austrian economy like in 1914?

The economy relied on agriculture and was industrially weak.

What was the Austrian military like in 1914?

The Austro-Hungarian army was large, but outdated and poorly equipped.

What was the population of Austria-Hungary in 1914?

The empire contained 52 million citizens but its weaknesses meant that it was difficult to control *(p.16)*.

DID YOU KNOW?

The Archduke Franz Ferdinand of Austria began his military career aged 12 and, unusually, married his wife for love, rather than for money or position.

THE OTTOMAN EMPIRE

The Turkish crescent.

What was the Ottoman Empire like in 1914?

The Ottoman Empire was the weakest of all of the Great Powers. It was known as the 'Sick Man of Europe'.

Where was the Ottoman Empire in 1914?

By 1914 *(p.23)* its empire had shrunk but it still contained some land in Europe, Turkey and the Middle East.

Who was the leader of the Ottoman Empire in 1914?

The head of state for the Ottoman Empire was Sultan Mehmed V. However, a coup in 1913 meant the empire was ruled by the Three Pashas on behalf of the army.

What was the economy of the Ottoman Empire like in 1914?

The empire was economically backwards with little modern infrastructure.

What was the foreign policy of the Ottoman Empire in 1914?

The Ottoman Empire had a number of foreign policy aims:

- ☑ The Ottoman Empire wanted to continue the Balkans Wars in order to regain control *(p.16)* of this region.
- ☑ The Young Turks were strongly nationalist and wanted Turkey to dominate other peoples in the Balkans region.

What was the population of the Ottoman Empire in 1914?

The empire contained 25 million subjects but was in serious decline and found it difficult to control *(p.16)* and rule over them.

DID YOU KNOW?

The Ottoman Empire fell in 1923; it had lasted for 623 years.

ITALY

The Italian wolf

What was Italy like in 1914?

Italy was among the weakest of the Great Powers in 1914.

What was Italy's foreign policy in 1914?

Italy had only been unified in 1870, therefore its foreign policy was focused on establishing Italy as a Great Power *(p.16)*:

- ☑ It joined the Dual Alliance, with Germany and Austria-German, thereby turning it into the Triple Alliance *(p.24)*, to gain recognition as a Great Power *(p.16)*.
- ☑ The country was poor, many citizens were illiterate and government corruption was widespread, which weakened its economic and military strength *(p.16)*.

- ✅ It claimed territories that were part of the Austro-Hungarian Empire where Italian-speaking people lived.
- ✅ It was part of the Triple Alliance *(p.24)* mainly because it wanted the support of Germany. It did not want to defend Austria-Hungary.

 ## What was the government of Italy like in 1914?

Italy was a constitutional monarchy with an elected parliament. The head of state was King Victor Emmanuel III.

 ## What was the population of Italy in 1914?

Italy had 35 million citizens, in addition to a number of subjects in its small overseas empire.

DID YOU KNOW?

Italy had been unified as a country since 1870, a year longer than Germany!

THE UNITED STATES OF AMERICA

The American eagle.

 ## What was the USA like in 1914?

The USA was not a major military power *(p.16)* in 1914, but it was an important economic rival to Europe.

 ## What was the government of the USA like in 1914?

The main features of the government of the USA were:

- ✅ A federal republic.
- ✅ A democratic state with much in common with Great Britain and France, although it did not support imperialism.
- ✅ The head of state was an elected president. From 1913 this was Woodrow Wilson, an idealist who believed in progressive ideas. He did not support autocrats.

 ## What was the economy of the USA like in 1914?

American industrial production was greater than Britain's and Germany's.

 ## What was the foreign policy of the USA in 1914?

The USA believed that it had the right to dominate the Americas and the Pacific region, but wished to stay out of European affairs.

 ## What was the population of the USA in 1914?

The USA was booming and European immigrants were adding to its rapidly growing population of 98 million citizens.

DID YOU KNOW?

The tune for the American national anthem is actually based on a drinking song, sung in pubs by English soldiers who fought against the Americans in the War of Independence.

THE TRIPLE ALLIANCE

A central European alliance.

What was the Triple Alliance?

The Triple Alliance was an agreement between Germany, Austria-Hungary and Italy, to provide military support to each other.

When was the Triple Alliance created?

The Triple Alliance was formed in May 1882.

Who was in the Triple Alliance?

The Triple Alliance consisted of three of Europe's great powers in 1914: Germany, Austria-Hungary and Italy.

Why was the Triple Alliance formed?

The Triple Alliance provided mutual support for the smaller countries; it was a chance to have a more powerful *(p. 16)* ally . For Germany, the alliance provided protection against encirclement by France and Russia.

DID YOU KNOW?

The Triple Alliance was originally called the Dual Alliance when agreed between Germany and Austria-Hungary in 1879. When Italy joined in 1882 it became the Triple Alliance.

THE TRIPLE ENTENTE

'Friendly agreements'.

What was the Triple Entente?

The Triple Entente was a military coalition between the Great Britain, France and Russia against any potential enemies.

When was the Triple Entente created?

The Triple Entente was created in 1907 when Russia joined Britain, who had previously united in the Entente Cordiale in 1904.

Who were members of the Triple Entente?

The Triple Entente consisted of three of Europe's great powers in 1914 - Russia, France and Great Britain.

Why was the Triple Entente formed?

The purpose of the Triple Entente was to protect its members against the growing threat of Germany and to support each other if there was a war.

Quizzes, amazing exam preparation tools and more at GCSEHistory.com

THE ASSASSINATION OF ARCHDUKE FRANZ FERDINAND, 1914

Death in Sarajevo.

What happened to Archduke Franz Ferdinand?

Archduke Franz Ferdinand, the heir to the Austro-Hungarian throne, was shot and fatally wounded.

Who killed Archduke Franz Ferdinand?

Gavrilo Princip, a member of the Black Hand, assassinated the archduke using a revolver.

Where was Archduke Franz Ferdinand assassinated?

Archduke Franz Ferdinand was assassinated in Sarajevo, the capital of Bosnia.

When was the assassination of Archduke Franz Ferdinand?

The assassination was carried out on 28th June, 1914.

Why was Archduke Franz Ferdinand assassinated?

Archduke Franz Ferdinand was assassinated by the Black Hand in an attempt to make sure he didn't pacify the Serbians in Bosnia. Pacifying the Serbians in Bosnia would strengthen the archduke's position when he came to the throne but would also undermine Serbia's plans to unite all Slavs in a Greater Serbia - the Black Hand wanted an independent Serbia, free from Austro-Hungarian and Ottoman rule.

What were the consequences of the assassination of Archduke Franz Ferdinand?

The main outcome of the assassination was the outbreak of the First World War. This happened in the aftermath of the assassination, during the 'July Days'.

THE JULY DAYS, 1914

The assassination led to a 'domino effect' as countries joined the war.

What were the 'July Days' before the outbreak of the First World War?

The July Days is the name given to the period between the assassination of Archduke Franz Ferdinand *(p.25)* and the start of the First World War.

What were the key events of the First World War 'July Days'?

The July Days are made up of 10 key exchanges between alliances;

- ☑ 28th June, 1914: Assassination of Franz Ferdinand.

- ☑ 5th July, 1914: Germany agreed to support Austria-Hungary in a potential conflict with Serbia. This is known as the 'blank cheque'.

- ☑ 23rd July, 1914: Austria-Hungary sent an ultimatum to Serbia.

- ☑ 25th July, 1914: Serbia agreed to all of Austria's demands except one.

- ☑ 26th July, 1914: Russia promised to support Serbia in any conflict.

- ☑ 28th July, 1914: Austria-Hungary declared war on Serbia. Serbia requested the support of Russia.

- ☑ 29th July, 1914: Germany warned Russia not to get involved but Russia mobilised its army. Two days later, Germany also warned France not to intervene.

- ☑ 1st August, 1914: Germany declared war on Russia and, in return, France mobilised its army.

- ☑ 2nd August, 1914: Germany requested access to Belgium, to attack France as part of the Schlieffen Plan *(p.26)*. Belgium refused. A day later, Germany declared war on France and invaded Belgium.

- ☑ 4th August, 1914: Britain declared war on Germany.

DID YOU KNOW?

The German Kaiser is infamous for issuing Austria-Hungary a 'blank cheque.' This means that he would support Austria no matter what action they took against Serbia in revenge for the assassination of Franz Ferdinand.

THE SCHLIEFFEN PLAN, 1914

The Germans had one inflexible plan of attack in the west and it quickly began to go wrong.

What was the Schlieffen Plan?

The Schlieffen Plan was a German war plan to avoid a war on two fronts by attacking France, travelling at high speed through Belgium. After defeating France, the German Army would then east turn and attack Russia.

When was the Schlieffen Plan created?

The plan was created in December 1905, though it was not employed until August 1914.

Who created the Schlieffen Plan?

The Schlieffen Plan was created by the most senior general in the German Army, Count Alfred von Schlieffen.

Why was the Schlieffen Plan created?

The plan was created in preparation for war due to growing rivalries at the time. Germany was particularly worried about being encircled by France and Russia.

 Why did the Schlieffen Plan fail?

The Schlieffen Plan failed for 6 key reasons:

- ☑ The Germans could not keep to the 6-week timetable for defeating France: the Belgian Army slowed the German advance at forts around Liege, while the BEF *(p.29)* slowed it further at the Battle of Mons *(p.30)*.

- ☑ The use of Plan 17, which was the French war plan to attack Germany's industrial centre, slowed the German advance by two weeks. However, the plan proved an overall failure for the French.

- ☑ Russian mobilisation came more quickly than expected and Russia invaded eastern Germany on 19th August. This caused Germany to send 100,000 troops to the east, weakening its attack against France.

- ☑ German supplies of food and ammunition could not keep up with the rapid advance, leaving soldiers tired, hungry and under-equipped.

- ☑ General von Kluck changed the plan. Instead of encircling Paris he decided to meet the French and British head on and aim to win a decisive victory at the Battle of the Marne *(p.31)*, but was defeated.

- ☑ At the Battle of the Marne *(p.31)* the Germans were forced back to the River Aisne where they began to dig trenches.

 What were the consequences of the failure of the Schlieffen Plan?

The failure of the Schlieffen Plan had 2 important consequences:

- ☑ It meant the Germans would now have to fight a war on two fronts, reducing their chance of victory.

- ☑ The Germans dug trenches to defend their captured territory. This led to the establishment of the Western Front and stalemate there until the summer of 1918.

DID YOU KNOW?

One of the reasons the Schlieffen Plan failed is that the march through Belgium was too slow. The Germans simply had too many soldiers crammed onto too few Belgian roads, causing massive traffic jams.

THE FRENCH ENTRY INTO THE WAR

France had no choice but to fight in August 1914.

 What made France enter the First World War?

Germany declared war against France as part of the Schlieffen Plan *(p.26)*.

 When did France join the First World War?

Germany declared war against France on the 3rd August 1914.

 Why did France join the First World War?

There were 3 main reasons for France joining the war:

- ☑ The Schlieffen Plan *(p.26)* assumed that France must be defeated if war with Russia began. As such Germany would need to declare war against France and defeat it before the Russians were ready to fight.

- ☑ The French Plan 17 involved an immediate attack across the Franco-German border into Alsace-Lorraine. This began the Battle of the Frontiers.
- ☑ The French used their massive fortresses along the border to launch attacks into Germany, while also sending troops to help the Belgian army trying to slow the German invasion of their territory.

DID YOU KNOW?

The Schlieffen Plan did not consider a situation where Germany would only fight Russia and not France. This meant that regardless of the situation, Germany would have to attack France.

THE BRITISH ENTRY INTO THE WAR

War for the sake of honour - Britain defends Belgium.

What made Britain enter the First World War?

When Germany invaded Belgium on 3rd August 1914 as part of the Schlieffen Plan *(p.26)*, Britain gave Germany an ultimatum to leave. Germany ignored it and Britain declared war.

When did Britain join the First World War?

Great Britain declared war on Germany on 4th August 1914.

Why did Britain join the First World War?

There were 3 main reasons for Britain joining the war:

- ☑ Britain had promised to defend Belgium in the 1839 Treaty of London. Kaiser Wilhelm II called it a 'scrap of paper' and did not believe Britain would honour it.
- ☑ Britain could not risk Germany gaining control *(p.16)* of ports on the English Channel. This would threaten Britain's overseas trade and empire.
- ☑ If Germany won the war, it would dominate Europe and become unbeatable. This would also threaten Britain's empire.

DID YOU KNOW?

Animals were on the front line of war, too. British people gave up their pet dogs to the army so that they could carry messages along the front line. Carrier pigeons were also used for this and the Germans even had trained soldiers to shoot them down.

THE BEF

Enter the British Expeditionary Force.

What was the BEF?

The British Expeditionary Force (BEF) was the home-based British army that would be sent to France to support the French.

What was the British Expeditionary Force like?

The BEF consisted of Britain's best trained and equipped professional soldiers. The force sent to France in August 1914 was made up of six infantry divisions and one cavalry division which numbered 150,000 men. The BEF was the smallest army of any of the Great Powers.

Who was in command of the British Expeditionary Force?

Field Marshal Sir John French *(p.93)* commanded until December 1915 when he was replaced by Field Marshal Sir Douglas Haig *(p.91)*, who led the BEF to victory in 1918.

What role did the British Expeditionary Force play in the war?

The BEF would take on the responsibility for Britain's military efforts on the Western Front. It would be expanded to include five armies in which over 5 million men would serve by 1918.

In which battles did the British Expeditionary Force fight?

The BEF fought in some of the largest battles of the war; Ypres 1915, the Somme *(p.45)* 1916, Arras 1917, Messines 1917, Passchendaele *(p.46)* 1917, Cambrai 1917, the Hundred Days Offensive 1918 and the Hindenburg *(p.95)* Line 1918.

What was the significance of the British Expeditionary Force?

The BEF would play a key role in defeating Germany in the final Hundred Days offensive of the war.

DID YOU KNOW?

Immediately on the outbreak of war, the British formed the Indian Expeditionary Force to support the BEF in France. The IEF set sail from India and landed in France on the 26th September 1914. Indian troops fought bravely in many of the major battles of 1914 and 1915, until they were sent to the Middle East in December 1915

BATTLE OF THE FRONTIERS, AUGUST-SEPTEMBER 1914

Plan 17 meets the Schlieffen Plan.

What was the Battle of the Frontiers?

The Battle of the Frontiers was a series of six major battles that took place shortly after the First World War began. For a short time the war was one of movement.

Which countries fought in the Battle of the Frontiers?

The Battle of the Frontiers was fought by the French, Belgian, British and German armies.

Where was the Battle of the Frontiers?

The battles took place along the French-German border, from Alsace-Lorraine to the Ardennes and southern Belgium.

 When was the Battle of the Frontiers?

The battles took place between the 4th August and the 6th September, 1914.

What were the main events of the Battle of the Frontiers?

There were six major battles that took place along the frontiers. This included the Battle of Mons *(p.30)* where the BEF *(p.29)* met the German Army for the first time and the French attack into Lorraine.

What was the significance of the Battle of the Frontiers?

The Battles of the Frontiers were significant for 4 reasons:

- ✅ The battles saw the Schlieffen Plan *(p.26)* and Plan 17 crash into each other. Both were designed to take the offensive against the other.

- ✅ The battles saw massed infantry attacks, with soldiers advancing in the open without cover. This resulted in massive casualties, with the French losing over 300,000 men.

- ✅ The French attacks into Germany failed and the Schlieffen Plan *(p.26)* was stopped at the Battle of the Marne *(p.31)* in September.

- ✅ The Allies and the Germans had learned that massed infantry attacks against machine guns and artillery *(p.42)* resulted in catastrophe. The war of movement was over and trench warfare developed. It would dominate the Western Front for the next four years.

DID YOU KNOW?

In 1914 some French units went into battle still wearing uniforms designed in the 19th Century. They had red trousers and caps, and blue coats, making them easy targets for German riflemen.

THE BATTLE OF MONS, AUGUST 1914

The British Expeditionary Force attempted to stop the German advance.

 What was the Battle of Mons?

The Battle of Mons was a significant event in the early days of the First World War, when the British Expeditionary Force *(p.29)* impeded, but failed to stop, the progress of the German Army as it advanced under the Schlieffen Plan *(p.26)*.

 When was the Battle of Mons?

The Battle of Mons took place on the 23rd August, 1914.

 What were the aims of each side at the Battle of Mons?

The BEF *(p.29)* was aiming to hold the line along the Mons canal, while the Germans aimed to continue their advance into France, while destroying the British and French forces that stood in their way.

Quizzes, amazing exam preparation tools and more at GCSEHistory.com

What strengths did the BEF have at the Battle of Mons?

The BEF *(p.29)* at Mons contained a force of about 75,000 men and 300 artillery *(p.42)* guns. Each battalion was armed with two Vickers machine-guns and there was an artillery brigade in each division. The men of the BEF were also expert and well-trained riflemen.

What strengths did the Germans have at the Battle of Mons?

The German troops at Mons were about 150,000 men and 600 artillery *(p.42)* guns. It was made up of eight divisions of the German 1st Army, with artillery and cavalry forces, and was part of the wider co-ordinated German advance into France.

What happened at the Battle of Mons?

The main events of the battle were:

- ☑ The British forces faced heavy bombardment by the Germans, who simultaneously attempted to outflank them on either side.
- ☑ British troops were forced to the south and west of Mons, and the Germans entered the town that evening. The next day, the British fell back.

What was the significance of the Battle of Mons?

The Battle of Mons was significant in a number of ways.

- ☑ It slowed down the German advance, although it failed to stop it.
- ☑ The British lost about 1,600 men. German losses were estimated at about 5,000.
- ☑ It demonstrated the potential of the BEF *(p.29)* to upset German plans. The kaiser had referred to the BEF as 'that contemptible little army', but afterwards a German general said that they were an 'incomparable army'.
- ☑ The retreat gave the British time to establish defences at the River Marne, where the next significant battle would take place.

DID YOU KNOW?

The riflemen in the British Expeditionary Force were so quick and skilful that the Germans believed that they were facing machine-guns.

THE BATTLE OF THE MARNE, SEPTEMBER 1914

The British and French soldiers combined to halt the German advance.

What was the Battle of the Marne?

The Battle of the Marne was the conflict in the early days of the First World War in which the advance of the German forces under the Schlieffen Plan *(p.26)* was halted, forcing both sides to dig in and fortify their positions with trenches.

When was the Battle of the Marne?

The Battle of the Marne took place between the 6th and the 10th September 1914.

Where did the Battle of the Marne take place?

The Battle of the Marne took place along the banks of the River Marne in France. In places, the fighting took occurred just 30 miles from Paris.

What happened at the Battle of the Marne?

The BEF *(p.29)*, after retreating from Mons, joined the French army in halting the German advance. The Germans fell back to the River Aisne and began to fortify their positions to prevent further retreat.

Why was the German advance stopped at the Battle of the Marne?

There were 2 main reasons why the Germans were stopped at the Marne:

- ☑ Some German soldiers had marched 150 miles and were exhausted from combat.
- ☑ They were held up because the French destroyed bridges and roads as they retreated.

What was the significance of the Battle of the Marne?

The Battle of the Marne was very significant to the outcome of the First World War:

- ☑ It halted the German advance into France, although the Germans continued to hold large areas of industrial north-east France.
- ☑ Both sides dug in to fortify their positions. This marked the beginning of trench warfare and of the stalemate that would last until 1918.

DID YOU KNOW?

The survivors of the 1914 BEF called themselves 'The Old Contemptibles'. This was after the German kaiser insulted the BEF by ordering his armies to 'walk over General French's contemptible little army.'

THE RACE TO THE SEA, SEPTEMBER-OCTOBER 1914

Both sides 'race for the sea'.

What was the Race to the Sea?

The Race to the Sea was an attempt by the British and French to outflank the northern wing of the German Army and attack its rear, after their defeat at the Battle of the Marne *(p.31)*. The 'race' only ended when the armies reached the North Sea coast.

Where was the Race to the Sea?

The Race to the Sea stretched for 125 miles. It started at the River Aisne in northern France and ended at the town of Nieuport on the North Sea coast of Belgium.

Which armies were involved in the Race to the Sea?

The Race to the Sea involved a combination of the British Expeditionary Force *(p.29)* (BEF), the French Second Army and the Belgian Army fighting against the German Second and Sixth Armies.

When was the Race to the Sea?

The Race to the Sea began around the 17th September and lasted until the 19th October 1914.

What were the key battles of the Race to the Sea?

There was a series of battles that made up the Race to the Sea:

- The First Battle of the Aisne (13th-28th September 1914). Dug in troops made frontal attacks impossible so the French, British and Germans tried to go around the newly dug trenches and began moving northward.

- The Battles of Picardy and Albert (22nd-29th September 1914) took place as the armies moved through the Somme *(p.45)* region of France, northwards towards Belgium.

- Battles of La Bassée, Messines and Armentières (10th October-2nd November 1914), were a series of battles in northern France which forced the British, French and German armies northwards towards the Belgian coast.

- The Battle of the Yser (18th October-30th November 1914) was the final battle of the race to sea. The Belgian army retreated from Antwerp and extra troops of the BEF *(p.29)* landed in Belgium to block the coast from a German advance.

What were the events of the Race to the Sea?

The 'Race to the Sea' was an attempt by the BEF *(p.29)* and French to outflank the German trenches along the River Aisne. This was a period of open warfare where both sides made wide use of their cavalry to move quickly ahead.

What were the outcomes of the Race to the Sea?

The 'Race to the Sea' is significant because it forced both sides to dig a line of unbroken trenches northwards to the coast. This line would become known as the Western Front and would stretch for 440 miles, from the North Sea to the Swiss border. Neither side could claim victory and it marked the beginning of trench warfare.

DID YOU KNOW?

At the start of the war unarmed reconnaissance planes were used to spy on enemy military positions. This played a key role in helping the allies win the Battle of the Marne, that began the Race for the Sea.

THE FIRST BATTLE OF YPRES, OCTOBER-NOVEMBER 1914

The British would hold on to the Ypres Salient throughout the rest of the war.

What happened at the First Battle of Ypres?

The Germans attacked the British positions to the east and north-east of Ypres.

When was the First Battle of Ypres?

The First Battle of Ypres was between 12th October and 11th November, 1914.

How many British died in the first battle of Ypres?

50,000 British troops were lost in this battle.

Who won the First Battle of Ypres?

The Germans won the battle, although the British did hold on to Ypres. This was important, as Ypres provided access to the ports to England, which meant that supplies could still be brought in.

THE TRENCH SYSTEM

Trench systems became quite sophisticated.

 What was the trench system?

Both sides dug networks of trenches to hold their positions on the Western Front. As they were developed they became more sophisticated, and became the soldiers' homes as well as where they fought.

 What were the key features of the trench system?

The trenches had 7 key features.

- ☑ Frontline trench. This was the first line of defence, and soldiers attacked from here.
- ☑ Support trench. This had support troops, and was also a place to retreat to if the front line was attacked and over-run.
- ☑ Reserve trench. This was sited 100m behind the support trench. Troops could rest here when they were not on the front line.
- ☑ Dugouts. These were holes, dug into the sides of trenches, where men could sleep or take cover.
- ☑ Communication trenches. These were used to connect the other trenches together.
- ☑ Trenches were cut in a zigzag pattern to stop bullets travelling a long way down them during an attack, or to stop explosions from travelling along the whole trench.
- ☑ No man's land. This was the space between the front lines of each side's trenches.

DEADLOCK ON THE WESTERN FRONT

Tactics and ineffective weapons led to a lack of progress for much of the war.

 What was deadlock (stalemate) on the Western Front?

The Western Front deadlock, or stalemate, was when both sides dug into their trenches from which they launched repeated attacks, resulting in very little gain and high numbers of casualties.

Why was there a deadlock on the Western Front?

There was deadlock on the Western Front due to a number of factors:

- The failure of the Schlieffen Plan *(p.26)*. As the Germans failed to advance, they dug in at places which were difficult to attack.
- The strength of defences *(p.16)*. Trenches were difficult to attack, especially as barbed wire and machine guns were used in defence.
- Ineffective weapons. Attacking weapons struggled against the strong defences early in the war, although weapons developed as the war progressed.
- The conditions. The geography of the Western Front made it difficult to fight. It was difficult to move across ground churned up by shellfire, or turned into muddy quagmires by heavy rain.
- No new tactics. Generals lacked experience in modern, industrialised war. They used old tactics such as cavalry charges and hand-to-hand fighting.

DID YOU KNOW?

The 'creeping' barrage was developed to help soldiers cross no-man's-land. The infantry would advance as close as they dared behind a curtain of shells falling in front of them.

LIFE IN THE TRENCHES

Casualties were caused by disease and illness as well as combat.

 How did people get ill in the First World War trenches?

Living and fighting in the trenches caused soldiers to suffer from a number of illnesses, mainly just from the awful conditions in the trenches.

 Why did the trenches make people ill?

The poor conditions, and persistent stress of living in the trenches, led to a number of physical and psychological illnesses.

 What common illnesses during the First World War were caused by life in the trenches?

Life in the trenches caused many illnesses, but 5 of the most important were:

- Shell shock *(p.36)*.
- Trench foot *(p.36)*.
- Trench fever *(p.37)*.
- Dysentery *(p.37)*.

☑ Gangrene. *(p.38)*

DID YOU KNOW?

Shell shock' was a name given for a new type of injury seen in the First World War. Men who had been under intense artillery bombardment could lose control of their bodies and minds as a result of this experience.

SHELL SHOCK

The effects of trench warfare had a psychological impact.

What was shell shock?

The stress of living and fighting in the trenches often caused psychological and mental health problems, known as 'shell shock'.

What were the symptoms of shell shock?

Shell shock could cause nightmares, loss of speech, uncontrollable shaking, and total mental breakdown.

What was the treatment for shell shock?

There was not much understanding about shell shock during the First World War. It was often seen as hysteria, or an attempt to get out of the war.

☑ Some men who suffered from shell shock were accused of cowardice, and punished.

☑ Attitudes towards those who suffered from shell shock could be harsh, and they were often accused of cowardice and malingering.

☑ Electric shock treatments were sometimes used.

☑ Many shell shock patients were cared for at home or sent to mental asylums.

☑ 2,000 men were treated for shell shock, including the poets Siegfried Sassoon and Wilfred Owen, at Craiglockhart Hospital in Scotland.

DID YOU KNOW?

306 British and Commonwealth soldiers were executed for desertion or cowardice during the war. It is now believed that many of these were suffering from shell shock.

TRENCH FOOT

Footcare became a priority.

What was trench foot?

Standing in cold, wet water led to a condition called trench foot, where the skin was soaked for such long periods of time that it began to rot. It was extremely painful and sometimes led to amputation of the foot.

How was trench foot prevented?

By 1915, the army understood that persistently cold, wet feet led to trench foot. Officials introduced several ways to try and prevent this.

- ☑ The feet were rubbed with whale oil to protect them.
- ☑ There were regular foot inspections by officers.
- ☑ Soldiers were instructed to change into clean, dry socks.

DID YOU KNOW?

A 'Blighty wound' was a wound that was serious enough to get you out of the trenches and sent back to Britain to recover.

TRENCH FEVER

Trenches were infested with lice and other vermin.

What was trench fever?

Trench fever affected up to half a million men, causing headaches, high temperatures, and flu-like symptoms.

What caused trench fever?

Rats and lice carried disease through the trenches.

How was trench fever prevented in the First World War?

By 1918, it was discovered that one way trench fever was spread was by lice; this led to the introduction of delousing stations.

DID YOU KNOW?

Soldiers would engage in 'chatting' - killing lice on their clothes. An effective method was to run a lighted candle over the places where they laid their eggs.

DYSENTERY

A disease caused by the unhygienic conditions in the trenches.

What caused dysentery in the First World War?

Dysentery spread because of the unhygienic latrines and lack of clean water in the trenches. It caused stomach pains, high temperature, diarrhoea, and even death from dehydration.

How was dysentery prevented in the First World War?

The army began to purify water by adding chloride of lime, but many soldiers didn't like the taste.

GANGRENE

Untended wounds could lead to severe infection.

? ### What caused gangrene in the First World War?

Gangrene is the death of body tissue, and occurs when blood supply cannot reach a wound, causing it to rot and produce a foul-smelling gas. It usually affects extremities such as toes, fingers and limbs.

 ### How did they treat gangrene in the First World War?

The only effective treatment for gangrene was amputation of the affected body part, to prevent it spreading and ultimately causing the patient's death.

DID YOU KNOW?

Dogs were trained to locate wounded or dying soldiers on the battlefield and to carry emergency medical supplies.

TREATMENT IN THE TRENCHES

The First World War saw the introduction of an effective medical evacuation system.

? ### What was the Royal Army Medical Corps?

Doctors and medics in the army belonged to the Royal Army Medical Corps, or RAMC. They worked in different stations on the Western Front.

 ### What was the chain of evacuation for the RAMC?

There was a 'chain of evacuation' to get wounded soldiers to a safe treatment area. The links in the chain were:

- ☑ Regimental Aid Posts (RAP).
- ☑ Dressing stations (ADS and MDS).
- ☑ Casualty Clearing Stations (CCS).
- ☑ Base hospitals.

DID YOU KNOW?

A British propaganda story claimed that the Germans operated Corpse Factories to boil down the bodies of their dead soldiers. It was designed to make the Germans appear barbarous. It was so convincing that several years after the war had ended people in Britain still believed it to be true.

Quizzes, amazing exam preparation tools and more at GCSEHistory.com

NEW WEAPONS AND METHODS

Killing technology improved.

What were the main weapons used in the First World War?

There were a number of new weapons and fighting methods introduced during the First World War. These included aircraft *(p.39)*, dogfights, machine guns, poisonous gas, tanks, and artillery. *(p.42)*

DID YOU KNOW?

Trench warfare was like a medieval siege. Both sides employed thousands of miners in special 'tunnelling' units to dig deep mines under each other's trenches.

AIRCRAFT

Aircraft developed rapidly during the war.

What was the role of aircraft in the First World War?

Aircraft were mostly used to gather intelligence on the enemy. This could be in the form of monitoring troop movements, trench layout or supply chains.

What were aircraft like in 1914?

In 1914 aeroplanes were extremely primitive, unarmed, unreliable and highly dangerous 'string bags'. Losses were very high, especially among new pilots.

How did aircraft improve during the war?

By 1918 aircraft were more specialised:

- ☑ 'Fighters' such as the Sopwith Camel were developed. These, were fitted with machine guns and were much faster and more maneuverable. Dogfights were common.
- ☑ 'Bombers', such as the German Gotha and the British Handley Page, had been designed that could carry heavy loads of bombs and drop them on distant targets.
- ☑ By 1918, 10,000 planes were being used and over 50,000 airmen had been killed.

What were dogfights in the First World War?

As aircraft were fitted with machine guns, they could fire on the men in the trenches and also against other enemy planes, in what became known as dogfights. These were spectacular aerial battles relying on a pilot's skill and reflexes.

What impact did aircraft have?

The war sped up the development of aircraft technology so they became a key weapon on the Western Front. Air power *(p.16)* was also used at sea to observe and attack shipping.

MACHINE GUNS

Machine guns were key to defence.

What was the role of machine guns in the First World War?

Machine guns were used to defend trenches throughout the war. A fairly new weapon, they could fire 400-600 bullets per minute with a range of up to 2,000 metres.

What were machine guns like in 1914?

The Germans had 12,000 in 1914, although the British did not use them in large numbers until 1915. They required a crew of four to six operators so they were more suited to defence than attack. They could rapidly overheat or jam.

How did machine guns improve during the war?

By 1918 they were widely used by all armies. The rate of fire had vastly increased and some handheld 'light machine guns' had been developed e.g. the Lewis gun, so could be used by attacking troops.

What impact did machine guns have?

They were one of the key defensive weapons of the war: devastatingly effective against infantry, they could cut down hundreds of advancing soldiers in minutes. However, they prolonged the stalemate rather than breaking it.

POISON GAS

Gas was a weapon of terror.

What was the role of poison gas in the First World War?

The role of gas was to try and help soldiers break into enemy trenches. Gas would cause terror or incapacitate the enemy. It was released from canisters into no-mans-land.

What was poison gas like in 1914?

Poison gas was not used in 1914 but introduced during the battles of 1915:

Quizzes, amazing exam preparation tools and more at GCSEHistory.com

- Chlorine gas was first used by the Germans at the Second Battle of Ypres in 1915.
- It was released into no-man's land from special canisters hidden in the front line.
- Thousands of French and Canadian soldiers suffocated or fled in terror from the choking green cloud.
- In revenge the British used chlorine gas at the Battle of Loos in September 1915. But winds blew the gas back into the British trenches, gassing more of the attacking troops than the Germans.
- During 1915, all sides began using phosgene and chlorine gas which suffocated and blinded soldiers.

How did poison gas improve during the war?

There were 3 key developments for poison gas during the war:

- By 1917, more lethal gases were developed e.g. mustard gas which burned the skin and lungs.
- Gas shells were introduced and fired at enemy lines to overcome earlier problems of wind direction.
- Specialised gas masks and protective clothing were developed for soldiers, dogs, horses and pigeons, all of whom served in the front lines and were at risk of gas attack.

What impact did poison gas have?

Gas was more of a psychological weapon and did not have a large impact on breaking the stalemate. Gas casualties made up only a small percentage of total casualties as scientists developed effective gas masks. Only 3,000 British troops were killed by gas.

DID YOU KNOW?

The poem 'Dulce et Decorum est' by Wilfred Owen describes a chlorine gas attack. Among some of the first improvised gas masks were urine soaked rags held over a soldiers mouth and nose. The urine or other liquid prevented the chlorine gas from being inhaled.

TANKS

'Lumbering slowly towards us came three huge mechanical monsters such as we had never seen before.' Bert Chaney, 1916.

What was the role of tanks in the First World War?

Tanks were used to cross difficult ground, destroy machine guns, provide cover for advancing infantry and crush barbed wire in front of enemy trenches. They allowed for quick advancement through the enemy trenches and beyond.

What were tanks like in 1914?

Tanks were used for the first time by the British at the Battle of the Somme *(p.45)* in 1916. They moved at walking pace, were not very manoeuvrable and were extremely unreliable - more than half broke down before they got to the German trenches. The Germans did not use tanks until 1918.

How did tanks improve during the war?

In November 1917 at Cambrai over 400 tanks were used and achieved great success. Unfortunately, they blasted through enemy lines so quickly that the infantry could not keep up.

What impact did tanks have?

Tanks were a key weapon in helping to break the stalemate. They were effective when used in great numbers, something that was only possible in the last year of the war.

DID YOU KNOW?

Tanks were grouped by gender! The first prototype tank (a male) was named 'Little Willie'. The difference between tank genders was that 'male' tanks were equipped with cannons, while 'female tanks' were equipped with machine guns.

ARTILLERY

Artillery was the weapon of the Western Front.

? What was the role of artillery in the First World War?

Artillery was used to bombard the enemy lines by firing huge shells (up to 108 kilograms) in preparation for an infantry attack. The aim was to destroy the barbed wire and the front line trenches which protected the wider trench system *(p.34)*.

What was artillery like in 1914?

In 1914 artillery use faced many challenges:

- ☑ In 1914 artillery was not very accurate & difficult to 'range' targets by spotting where the shells landed. There was no way for infantry to effectively communicate with the 'gunners' (artillery) from the front line.
- ☑ Firing from well behind their own lines, artillery sometimes bombarded their own forward trenches because they could not see where their shells landed.
- ☑ By 1915 as many as 50% of British shells were 'duds'.
- ☑ Factories could not produce enough shells. The British fired 250,000 shells at the Battle of Loos in 1915 but they called off the attack partly because of a shortage of artillery shells.

How did artillery improve during the war?

From 1915 major improvements took place in the use of artillery:

- ☑ Shells improved in quality and quantity meaning many fewer 'duds'; in 1916 'fuse 106' was developed by the British, which was far more effective at cutting barbed wire.
- ☑ Howitzers were improved and more widely used. These fired shells high in the air and so could drop shells into trenches accurately, even if they could not be seen by the gunners.
- ☑ New tactics had been introduced e.g. the creeping barrage and the box barrage.
- ☑ Spotter aircraft *(p.39)*, spotter balloons and radio were being used to send live information to the artillery about where and what to fire at.

What impact did artillery have?

Artillery bombardments caused more casualties than any other weapon. It was a key weapon of the war.

TUNNELLING AND MINING

The German troops were stunned, dazed and horror-stricken if they were not killed outright. Many of them lay dead in the great craters opened by the mines.' Sir Philip Gibbs

What was the role of tunnelling in the First World War?

Special tunnelling companies were formed to try and break the stalemate of trench warfare. They tunnelled under enemy trenches and laid huge amounts of explosives in order to blow holes in the front line, ahead of an attack.

What was tunnelling like in 1914?

Tunnelling began as a reaction to the dangers of advancing across no-mans-land and quickly became an important battlefield tactic.

- As soon as trench warfare began, all sides began digging, creating interlinked underground complexes of trenches and dugouts.
- The French were the very first to use tunnels and exploding mines against the Germans in October 1914.
- The Germans first used tunnels and mines to attack Indian troops in December 1914. The British then copied this and formed their own tunnelling companies.

How did tunnelling improve during the war?

Tunnelling developed to become an important tactic in trench warfare. There were a number of key developments:

- By 1916, the British had over 25,000 tunnellers, many of them recruited from miners who knew how to dig underground.
- Some tunnels and mines were huge and could take up to a year to dig before an offensive.
- At the Battle of Messines in 1917, the British prepared 20 mines with 600 tonnes of explosives. They dug over 8,000 metres of tunnel.
- The Messines mines were exploded in a period of 20 seconds, killing over 10,000 German defenders.
- The detonation of the mines was a huge success as they blew a hole in the German defences and allowed Messines Ridge to be captured without high casualties.

What impact did tunnelling have?

Tunnel warfare had the following 2 effects on trench warfare:

- Mines caused fear in defending troops who lived with the knowledge that the enemy was digging under them and planting huge mines that could kill them. It added to the psychological impact of the war.
- Mines could open up the front lines but could not help the attacker break through deep lines of trenches. It failed to end trench warfare and had to be used in combination with other, newer tactics to be effective.

THE BATTLE OF VERDUN, FEBRUARY - DECEMBER 1916

'Bleed the French white' was the German plan for Verdun.

What was the Battle of Verdun?

The Battle of Verdun was a major battle between French and German forces on the Western Front.

What happened at the Battle of Verdun?

The main events of the battle were:

- ☑ The Germans attacked and initially made good progress, capturing the forts around the town.
- ☑ French soldiers counterattacked and pushed the Germans back. After several months the German attacks petered out.

When was the Battle of Verdun?

The Battle of Verdun was the longest battle of the First World War, lasting from the 21st January 1916 until the 18th December 1916.

Where was the Battle of Verdun?

The Battle of Verdun was fought in a salient around the French town of Verdun. This was chosen as it was of symbolic importance to the French, and the Germans knew the French would fight hard to defend it.

Why did the Germans attack at the Battle of Verdun?

General Erich von Falkenhayn wanted to 'bleed France white'. The aim was to kill more French soldiers than German, causing the French army to collapse. This is known as a war of attrition.

What were the consequences of the Battle of Verdun?

The Battle of Verdun had 2 main results;

- ☑ Both the French and German armies were weakened.
- ☑ Verdun was saved.

Why did the German attack at the Battle of Verdun fail?

The Battle of Verdun is seen as a German failure for 3 key reasons;

- ☑ The German plan of attrition had failed as they had almost as many casualties (350,000) as the French (400,000).
- ☑ The French appointed General Petain to defend the city. He told the French troops that the Germans 'shall not pass' and ordered the pouring of men and equipment into the Verdun salient along 'the Sacred Way'.
- ☑ In July, the Allies launched their own offensives: the British at the Somme *(p.45)* and the Russians on the Eastern Front. This meant Germany had to pull troops out of Verdun to defend other areas.

Quizzes, amazing exam preparation tools and more at GCSEHistory.com

THE BATTLE OF THE SOMME, JULY - NOVEMBER 1916

An Anglo-French effort to break the stalemate.

What was the Battle of the Somme?

The Battle of the Somme was fought by British and French forces against the Germans. It was part of an offensive to force the Germans back and achieve victory on the Western Front.

When was the Battle of the Somme?

The battle took place from 1st July, 1916 to 18th November, 1916.

Where was the Battle of the Somme?

It took place on the River Somme in France, where the British and French armies met.

Why was the Somme Offensive launched?

It was part of an offensive to force the Germans back and achieve victory on the Western Front. It was also launched to help relieve pressure on the French, who were under attack at Verdun *(p.44)* to the south.

What were the consequences of the Battle of the Somme?

The battle had 4 key outcomes;

- ☑ On the first day of the battle there were up to 57,000 British casualties compared with the Germans' 8,000. Haig *(p.91)* continued the attack and, by November, casualties numbered 620,000 for the Allies and 450,000 for the Germans.
- ☑ At most, the Allies advanced by 15km along just part of the Western Front. The expected breakthrough never occurred.
- ☑ However, the Germans called off their attacks at Verdun *(p.44)*, saving the French army there.
- ☑ The Allies developed new technology (the tank *(p.41)*) and tactics (the creeping barrage), which contributed to victory later.

Why was the Battle of the Somme unsuccessful?

The battle is seen as an Allied failure for 3 main reasons:

- ☑ The Germans knew the attack was coming due to aerial reconnaissance. They moved away from the front line into strengthened trenches, some as deep as 12 metres.
- ☑ In the week before the attack, 1.73 million shells were fired at the German lines. However, they were not effective in destroying German dugouts or cutting the barbed wire. Additionally, over a third of those shells fired were 'duds' and failed to explode.
- ☑ Following the bombardment of shells, General Haig *(p.91)* told soldiers to advance slowly towards the enemy trenches. He believed they would be undefended; but they were not, and heavy casualties occurred.

THE BATTLE OF PASSCHENDAELE, JULY - NOVEMBER 1917

The battle can be summed up as 'mud and blood'.

What was the Battle of Passchendaele?

The Battle of Passchendaele was a joint British and Canadian offensive against the Germans, led by General Haig *(p.91)*.

When was the Battle of Passchendaele?

The battle began in July 1917 and finished on 10th November 1917.

Where was the Battle of Passchendaele?

The battle took place in Passchendaele in the Ypres Salient.

What were the aims of the Battle of Passchendaele?

Haig *(p.91)* wanted to break through German lines and control *(p.16)* the coast. He wanted to capture naval bases to make it harder for the Germans to carry out submarine attacks on British ships.

What were the results of the Battle of Passchendaele?

There were 3 key outcomes from the battle:

- ☑ After three months of fighting, Passchendaele was captured and Haig *(p.91)* could claim victory.
- ☑ The battle came at a cost. A total of 240,000 British and 220,000 German soldiers were wounded or killed.
- ☑ In total, the Allies captured around 8km of territory, and Haig *(p.91)* failed to achieve his main objective.

Why did the Battle of the Passchendaele fail?

There were 2 main reasons why the battle plan failed:

- ☑ As with the Somme *(p.45)*, the Germans were aware of the coming attack.
- ☑ Heavy rains turned the battlefield into a quagmire. Soldiers were knee-deep in liquid mud, making it difficult to move.

THE GERMAN THREAT IN THE NORTH SEA

The war at sea repeated the stalemate of the Western Front.

What was the German naval threat?

Britain had the largest navy in 1914 but, due to the naval arms race, Germany offered a serious challenge. The two navies acted as a mutual deterrent, as both sides wanted to retain their fleets and avoid any major damage. This meant there was also a stalemate at sea for most of the war.

> **DID YOU KNOW?**
>
> During the war, the Germans built 360 U-boats, of which 176 were sunk.

THE BATTLE OF HELIGOLAND BIGHT, AUGUST 1914

Opening shots of the naval war.

What was the Battle of Heligoland?

The Battle of Heligoland was a British attack on German destroyers in the North Sea.

What happened during the Battle of Heligoland?

A British squadron of 31 destroyers, two cruisers and eight submarines attacked a German patrol.

When was the Battle of Heligoland?

The battle took place on 28th August, 1914.

What were the results of the Battle of Heligoland?

There were 3 key outcomes to the battle;

- ☑ Three German cruisers and one destroyer were sunk, with three more cruisers badly damaged. It also resulted in the death of 712 German sailors, with 530 injured and 336 taken prisoner.
- ☑ Britain suffered damage to one cruiser and three destroyers. 35 sailors were killed with a further 40 injured.
- ☑ The German kaiser was angry at the loss of ships and ordered that any future action must first be approved by him. This meant there was no major fleet action for several months after Heligoland.

> **DID YOU KNOW?**
>
> The Royal Navy kept a blockade of all German ports until mid-1919. It is estimated that this blockade led to the deaths of 424,000 German civilians from 1914-1919.

GERMAN RAIDS

British civilians were shelled for the first time.

What were German raids?

The German raids were attacks on British ships and towns.

Why were there German raids on Britain in the First World War?

The German raids had 3 main aims:

- ☑ To plant mines that would sink British ships.
- ☑ To create an ambush scenario, where British ships would chase German ships nearer to the German coast before being attacked by reinforcements.
- ☑ To split up the British fleet into smaller units as they went to defend coastal towns. This would leave the British ships isolated and easier to attack.

When were the German raids?

The Germans carried out two big coastal raids on the English coastline on November 3rd and December 16th, 1914.

Where did the German raids occur?

The Germans bombarded Great Yarmouth in November and then in December they bombarded Scarborough, Whitby and Hartlepool.

What were the results of the German raids?

The Germans were able to lay mines easily at Yarmouth. At Scarborough, shelling took place that destroyed property and killed more than 100 people.

THE BATTLE OF DOGGER BANK, JANUARY 1915

Success for the Royal Navy.

What was the Battle of Dogger Bank?

The Battle of Dogger Bank was a naval battle in the North Sea between Britain and Germany.

What happened during the Battle of Dogger?

The British learned of an attack in the North Sea and sent a fleet to surprise the Germans. The Germans turned back and the British chased them. The British attacked the fleet, focusing mainly on the German cruiser, Blücher.

When was the Battle of Dogger?

The battle took place on 24th January, 1915.

What were the results of the Battle of Dogger?

The British sank the German cruiser, Blücher, resulting in the deaths of 954 men. Britain didn't lose any ships, although 15 men were killed.

THE BATTLE OF JUTLAND, MAY 1916

The largest naval battle of the war.

What was the Battle of Jutland?

The Battle of Jutland was the largest naval battle of the First World War, between Britain and Germany off the coast of Denmark.

What happened during the Battle of Jutland?

The Germans intended to draw out the British fleet and make a surprise attack. However, the British already knew of the plan and had sent its fleet ready to attack 259 warships, with 100,000 men on board, fought at Jutland.

When was the Battle of Jutland?

The battle took place between 31st May and 1st June 1916.

What were the results of the Battle of Jutland?

The British suffered the most damage, with 14 ships and 6,000 lives lost. Germany only lost nine ships and 2,500 men. However, both sides claimed victory as, while the Germans had sunk more ships, the German fleet never again left port for fear of being destroyed. Britain continued to control *(p.16)* the North Sea.

SUBMARINE WARFARE

The use of U-boats posed a serious threat to Britain.

What was submarine warfare?

Submarine warfare was conducted by the Germans using U-boats to destroy merchant navy ships.

How many ships did Germany sink using submarine warfare?

U-boats were German submarines which were used to sink enemy ships. In 1915, Germany had 21 U-boats and sank 4% of ships supplying Britain, despite the target being to destroy all merchant shipping. By 1917, the number of German U-boats had increased to 200, and they sank 841,114 tonnes of Allied shipping that year.

 ### What tactics did Germany use in U-boat warfare?

The Germans sank all ships entering British waters, regardless of which country they belonged to, until the sinking of the Lusitania *(p.51)* in 1915 almost brought the USA into the war. This was known as unrestricted U-boat warfare. The policy was abandoned until 1917 when an increasingly desperate Germany tried it again, leading the USA to declare war on Germany.

 ### Why did the Germans use submarine warfare?

U-boats were used to destroy merchant ships bringing in food and war materials from abroad. This was in retaliation for the naval blockade of German ports by Britain.

 ### How effective was submarine warfare?

Overall, Germany's U-boat campaign did not have the desired effect:

- ☑ Although reduced to six weeks' food supply by 1917, the people of Britain did not starve due to rationing and anti U-boat measures.
- ☑ Likewise, the sinking of American ships brought the USA into the war in April 1917.

DID YOU KNOW?

The word U-boat comes from the German 'unterseeboot', meaning underwater boat.

ANTI U-BOAT MEASURES

Tackling the U-boat threat.

 ### What were anti U-boat measures?

Britain was in danger of losing the war because the shipping which the country relied on was being sunk by German submarines, or U-boats. Countering the U-boat threat was seen as a very important task.

 ### What anti U-boat measures did the British use in the First World War?

There were 4 main anti U-boat measures brought in by the British to try and avoid the damage being done by German U-boats;

- ☑ Minefields were laid across the English Channel and in the North Sea. If a U-boat collided with a mine it would be destroyed.
- ☑ Depth charges were introduced. These were explosives which were dropped by the British and exploded at certain depths.
- ☑ A convoy system was introduced. This meant merchant ships carrying supplies sailed in groups protected by the Royal Navy.
- ☑ Q-ships were introduced. These were warships which looked like merchant ships but they were actually armed and could fight the U-boats.

How successful were British anti U-boat measures?

The anti-U-boat measures were extremely successful for a number of reasons:

- ☑ Mines were highly effective. In 1917 alone, 20 out of 63 U-boats were sunk after they collided with mines.
- ☑ As crews became more experienced with using depth charges, they became more effective. In 1915 only five U-boats were sunk in this way, but the number reached 22 by 1917.
- ☑ Convoys were extremely successful, with only 1% of ships in convoy being destroyed.
- ☑ Q-ships attacks accounted for 10% of all U-boats sunk.

DID YOU KNOW?

Frederick Parslow won a Victoria Cross after a U-boat attacked his merchant ship. He single-handedly steered the ship until he was killed by a shell. His actions saved his ship, over 1,000 army horses and most of his crew. As a civilian in the merchant marine he was not eligible for the V.C. but the Royal Navy made him an honorary officer. At the age of 59, he is also the oldest recipient of the award.

THE SINKING OF THE LUSITANIA

The sinking caused Germany to change its approach.

 What happened to the Lusitania?

The Lusitania was a British civilian cruise liner that was sunk by a German U-boat.

 When was the Lusitania sunk?

The attack took place on 7th May, 1915.

 How was the Lusitania sunk?

The Lusitania departed New York, bound for Liverpool. However, it was torpedoed just 13km from the coast of Ireland by the U20, a German U-boat. The ship sank within 18 minutes.

 Who was on the Lusitania?

There were 1,959 passengers on board. Of the 1,198 who drowned, 128 were American.

 Why did the Germans sink the Lusitania?

The Germans attacked the Lusitania as there were war materials on board. This made sinking the ship justifiable in the context of war.

 What were the reactions to the sinking of the Lusitania?

There was international outrage at the sinking. Britain and America protested and there were calls for America to declare war on Germany. America issued a warning to Germany but did not declare war at that time.

THE GALLIPOLI CAMPAIGN, 1915

The campaign was an attempt to break the stalemate of the Western Front.

What was the Gallipoli campaign?

The campaign was an Allied attempt to open up another campaign and to draw German forces away from the Western front.

What were the aims of the Gallipoli campaign?

In October 1914, Turkey joined forces with Germany and Austria-Hungary. As Turkey controlled the Dardanelles, which connected the Mediterranean Sea to the Black Sea, Britain could no longer send supplies to Russia, and Russian ships in the Black Sea were trapped. The Gallipoli campaign was needed to:

- ☑ Supply Russia through the Black Sea ports.
- ☑ Break the stalemate on the Western Front *(p.35)* by drawing in German forces to support its weaker ally, Turkey.

Who was in charge of the Gallipoli campaign?

It was an Anglo-French operation led by Winston Churchill, the British first lord of the Admiralty.

When was the Gallipoli campaign?

The campaign ran from February 1915 to January 1916.

Where was the Gallipoli campaign?

At Gallipoli, in northwest Turkey.

What happened during the Gallipoli campaign?

There were a number of events during the Gallipoli campaign:

- ☑ On 19th February, 1915, Anglo-French naval forces began to bombard Turkish positions along the coast. 18th March, 1915 saw the main attack launched, but the fleet retreated after losing three battleships.
- ☑ After the retreat, the decision was taken to launch a ground invasion. Allied troops landed on 25th April, 1915, with the aim of capturing the forts that guarded the entrance to the Dardanelles.
- ☑ The naval attack warned the Turks of the planned invasion, so they were prepared and had strengthened their positions since February 1915.
- ☑ Allied troops landed at Anzac Cove under heavy fire, but established themselves. However, they were unable to move inland and a stalemate developed.
- ☑ The Allies withdrew between 10th December, 1915 and 9th January, 1916. Over 135,000 Allied troops were evacuated. This was the most successful part of the campaign, with only three casualties recorded.

What were the results of the Gallipoli campaign?

There were 5 important consequences of the failed campaign:

- ✅ 204,000 Allied troops were wounded and 48,000 killed.
- ✅ Many soldiers became ill, due to the poor living conditions.
- ✅ The Dardanelles were not captured, and this meant Russia was cut off from Allied support.
- ✅ Germany was able to strengthen its Western Front position as the Allies looked to make gains in Gallipoli.
- ✅ Churchill and Hamilton (the leaders of the campaign) were removed from their positions.

DID YOU KNOW?

ANZAC stands for Australian and New Zealand Army Corps. Their actions at Gallipoli are commemorated in Australia and New Zealand every year on 25 April.

THE ARMENIAN GENOCIDE

The first modern genocide.

What was the Armenian Genocide?

The Armenian genocide was the deliberate deportation and murder of Armenian subjects of the Ottoman Empire. This resulted in the deaths of up to 1.5 million Armenians.

Who committed the Armenian Genocide?

The 'Young Turks' movement seized power *(p. 16)* in 1908 and aimed to make Turkey the dominant culture. They used the Ottoman government and the military to plan and carry out the deportations and massacres.

Where did the Armenian Genocide take place?

The killings took place across Turkey. Many Armenians were also sent on death marches into the deserts of Mesopotamia (in modern-day Iraq and Syria).

When did the Armenian Genocide happen?

The genocide began on 24th April, 1915 with the first deportation of Armenian men, and ended in 1923.

What was the significance of the Armenian Genocide?

The genocide is significant in a number of ways:

- ✅ It had a devastating effect on the Armenian population of Turkey. Nearly all Armenians in Turkey were killed or expelled.
- ✅ When the Ottoman Empire collapsed in 1918, it led to the creation of Turkey through a process of violent nationalism.
- ✅ Further massacres of Armenians, Greeks and other minorities continued into 1921, even as the Big Three applied the Treaty of Sevres to Turkey after the First World War had ended.

DID YOU KNOW?

Even today, the Turkish government officially denies that a genocide occurred against the Armenians in the period 1916-1921.

THE BALFOUR DECLARATION

Britain promises a Jewish homeland.

What was the Balfour Declaration?

The Balfour Declaration was a statement issued by the British Government in November 1917.

What was written in the Balfour Declaration?

It related to Palestine which was a territory of the Ottoman Empire. It was designed to win American support for the war and undermine Ottoman control *(p.16)* of the region. It had 3 main aspects:

- ☑ It pledged British support for the establishment of a Jewish homeland in Palestine.
- ☑ It did not state what this homeland would look like.
- ☑ It stated that 'nothing shall be done which may prejudice the civil and religious rights of existing non-Jewish communities in Palestine, or the rights and political status enjoyed by Jews in any other country.'.

When was the Balfour Declaration?

The Balfour Declaration was signed by the British foreign secretary, Arthur Balfour, on 2nd November, 1917.

What were the causes of the Balfour Declaration?

The Balfour Declaration happened for several reasons:

- ☑ Members of the British government believed good relations with the Jews were key to winning the war.
- ☑ There were numerous British politicians and public figures who were sympathetic towards the Zionists and their ambitions.
- ☑ The British and French had agreed to divide the Ottoman Empire between them in 1915, and had decided a state should be created in Palestine.
- ☑ The British believed relations between Jews and Arabs could be managed if the rights of all religious groups were respected.

What were the results of the Balfour Declaration?

There were 3 main consequences of the Balfour Declaration:

- ☑ Tensions between Arab and Jewish communities rose during the 1920s and resulted in several violent clashes.
- ☑ The most significant result was mass Jewish immigration from Europe during the 1920s and 1930s.
- ☑ The Balfour Declaration offered few real guarantees to the Palestinian Arabs.

DID YOU KNOW?

Lawrence of Arabia, the British officer who helped to successfully lead the Arab revolt from 1916 to 1918, never had one day of military training or experience.

Quizzes, amazing exam preparation tools and more at GCSEHistory.com

OTTOMAN DEFEAT
The 'sick man of Europe'.

How did the war end for the Ottoman Empire?
The Ottoman Empire requested an armistice with Britain.

Which countries were involved in the defeat of the Ottoman Empire?
The Ottoman Empire had fought, Britain, France, Russia, Greece and the Arabs of the Middle East.

When was the Ottoman Empire defeated?
The Ottomans signed an armistice on the 30th October, 1918.

Why was the Ottoman Empire defeated?
There were a number of reasons why the Ottoman Empire had to admit defeat:

- The British invaded Iraq and captured Baghdad in 1917 and the oil fields of Mosul in 1918.
- The Arabs rose up in revolt with the help of the British in 1916. They invaded Jordan and helped to destroy the Ottoman Army in Palestine and Syria in 1918.
- The British invaded Palestine and captured Jerusalem in 1917.
- The Russians fought the Ottoman Empire in the Caucasus losing many soldiers and territory until 1917, when Russia pulled out of the war due to the Bolshevik Revolution.
- By 1918 there were large scale desertions from the Ottoman army.

DID YOU KNOW?

The British raised the Imperial Camel Corps to fight in the Middle East against the Ottomans. It was made up of British, Australian, New Zealand and Indian soldiers, all riding camels.

THE RUSSIAN ENTRY INTO THE WAR
'They are fighting a war for the purpose of retaining the colonies they have grabbed and robbed.'
Vladimir Lenin.

What happened with Russia and the First World War when it joined?
Russia joined with Britain and France in the Triple Entente *(p.24)*, against Germany and the Triple Alliance *(p.24)*, in the First World War.

When did Russia enter the First World War?
Germany declared war on Russia on 1st August, 1914. Russia ended the war with Germany on 3rd March, 1918.

Why did Russia enter the First World War?
There were 2 key reasons why Russia entered the First World War:

- Austria declared war on Serbia on the 28th July, 1914. Russia mobilised her troops in July to protect Serbia.

☑ Germany declared war on Russia because Russia refused to stop mobilising her troops.

 What was the public response to Russia's entry into the First World War?

There were 3 main initial responses:

☑ The people of the Russian Empire were very patriotic and supported Nicholas II.

☑ The Duma and constitutions, while they were in reality very limited in the freedoms they granted, placated the nationalities and prevented any mass uprisings.

☑ The tsar became more popular as the military was initially successful against Germany.

 How successful was Russia's military when they entered the First World War?

There were 3 key military defeats:

☑ Germany defeated Russia at Tannenberg *(p.57)* in August 1914.

☑ Germany defeated Russia at Masurian Lakes in September 1914.

☑ Russia had done incredibly badly by the end of 1915. The Germans had occupied parts of Russia and 2 million men were dead or injured.

 Why did discontent grow when Russia entered the First World War?

There were 3 main reasons for growing discontent connected to the First World War:

☑ The military defeats and the German occupation.

☑ The people blamed Nicholas II and his government for the failures and the poor state of the Russian Army which had insufficient supplies.

☑ The First World War exacerbated the extreme domestic impoverishment.

 When did Tsar Nicholas II take command of Russia's army in the First World War?

Tsar Nicholas II took command of the Russian army and navy in August 1915.

 Why did Tsar Nicholas II take command of Russia's war effort during the First World War?

Nicholas II thought it was his duty to take command, especially as the army had suffered several key defeats.

 What were the consequences of Tsar Nicholas II taking command of Russia's war effort during the First World War?

The decision of Tsar Nicholas II to assume command of the Russian Army was widely seen as a mistake for 3 key reasons:

☑ People now blamed him personally for Russia's military defeats.

☑ It caused his popularity with the people to decrease.

☑ He left Tsarina Alexandra in control *(p.16)* as regent and she was extremely unpopular.

DID YOU KNOW?

Unlike the Western Front, the Eastern Front was one of movement due to the much larger distances over which the different armies marched.

THE BATTLE OF TANNENBERG, AUGUST 1914

The Russian steamroller invades East Prussia.

What happened at Tannenberg?

The Battle of Tannenberg occurred after two Russian armies invaded Germany. It was the first major battle of the Eastern Front and resulted in a major German victory.

Which armies fought at Tannenberg?

The Battle of Tannenberg was fought between the German Eighth Army defending East Prussia, and the Russian First and Second Armies.

In which region did the Battle of Tannenberg take place?

The Battle of Tannenberg took place in East Prussia.

When was Battle of Tannenberg?

The Battle of Tannenberg took place between the 26th and the 30th August, 1914.

Who commanded the German Army at the Battle of Tannenberg?

The German forces were led by Field Marshal Paul von Hindenburg *(p.95)* and his Chief of Staff, Erich Ludendorff.

What was the significance of Battle of Tannenberg?

The Germans were outnumbered and von Hindenburg *(p.95)* and Ludendorff became national heroes for saving East Prussia from the Russian invasion. One Russian division was completely destroyed and the other retreated back to Poland. The Russians did not recover from this defeat until 1915.

DID YOU KNOW?

The use of radio communications was becoming important in war. This was revealed when Russian generals used unencrypted messages on their radios. The Germans intercepted them and knew exactly what the Russian plan of attack was.

THE BATTLE OF THE MASURIAN LAKES, SEPTEMBER 1914

The Germans win the initiative on the Eastern Front.

What happened at the Masurian Lakes?

The Battle of the Masurian Lakes took place straight after the victory at Tannenberg *(p.57)*. It was an attempt by the Germans to finally push the Russians out of their territory and end the threat to East Prussia.

Which armies fought at the Masurian Lakes?

The battle was between the German Eight Army and the Russian First and Tenth Armies.

In which region did the Battle of the Masurian Lakes take place?

The Battle of Masurian Lakes took place in East Prussia, which is in present-day Poland.

When was the Battle of the Masurian Lakes?

The Battle of the Masurian Lakes took place between the 7th and 14th September, 1914.

Who commanded the German Army at the Battle of the Masurian Lakes?

The German forces were led by Field Marshal Paul von Hindenburg *(p.95)* and his Chief of Staff, Erich Ludendorff.

What were the consequences of the Battle of the Masurian Lakes?

One Russian division was completely destroyed and all Russian forces were pushed out of East Prussia. However, German troops had been moved from the Western Front to help. This ended any chance of the Schlieffen Plan *(p.26)* working and resulted in the German defeat at the Battle of the Marne *(p.31)*.

DID YOU KNOW?

Due to the great distances on the Eastern Front, both the Russian and Austro-Hungarian armies used armoured trains. Some were so big that they carried naval guns and heavy artillery.

THE BRUSILOV OFFENSIVE, JUNE - SEPTEMBER 1916

The Russians pull off one of the greatest victories of the war.

What was the Brusilov Offensive?

The Brusilov Offensive was the largest offensive of the war. It was launched by Russia against mainly Austro-Hungarian forces on the Eastern Front.

Which armies participated in the Brusilov Offensive?

The Brusilov Offensive was a massive attack by four Russian Armies against the Austro-Hungarian forces. Later, German forces would also be sent to help their ally.

Where did the Brusilov Offensive take place?

The Brusilov Offensive took place over a 300 mile section of the Eastern Front in Western Ukraine, Poland and East Prussia.

When was the Brusilov Offensive?

The Brusilov Offensive took place from the 4th June until the 20th September, 1916. It lasted for 3 months and sixteen days.

Who commanded the forces in the Brusilov Offensive?

The commander of the Russian forces was General Aleksei Brusilov *(p.93)*. The Austro-Hungarian forces were commanded by Field Marshal Franz Conrad von Hötzendorf. German troops were commanded by Field Marshal Paul von Hindenburg *(p.95)*.

What was the significance of the Brusilov Offensive?

The Brusilov Offensive was the greatest victory of the Triple Entente *(p.24)* and one of the most bloody battles in history. It almost destroyed the Austro-Hungarian forces on the Eastern Front. It was Russia's greatest victory, but the vast scale of losses - at least 500,000 Russians died - contributed to Russia's collapse in 1917.

DID YOU KNOW?

The Eastern Front was at least 1,600 kilometres long, compared to the 700 kilometres of the Western Front.

THE FEBRUARY REVOLUTION, 1917

The revolutions of 1917 were triggered by Russia's involvement in the First World War.

 What was the February Revolution?

The February Revolution was the first of two revolutions which took place in Russia in 1917. The February Revolution began with strikes and riots over the lack of food.

 When was the February Revolution?

The February Revolution is sometimes known as the March Revolution depending on which calendar is used. It took place between 23rd February and 3rd March, 1917, using the old calendar, or between 8th and 16th March, 1917, using the new one.

 Where did the February Revolution take place?

The February Revolution of 1917 occurred in Petrograd. Petrograd, located on the Baltic Sea in the north-west of Russia, was called St Petersburg until 1914. It was then renamed, as it was felt the original name was 'too German'. It became Leningrad in 1924, after Lenin's death, and was then renamed St Petersburg once again in 1991.

 What caused the February Revolution?

There were several immediate and long-term causes of the February Revolution.

 What were the long-term causes of the February Revolution?

There were 4 key long-term causes:

- ☑ The discontent caused by the awful living and working conditions of the working class.
- ☑ The discontent caused by poverty and the frequent hunger suffered by peasants. There were also continuing issues with land ownership.
- ☑ Middle class anger and frustration at not having any real political power *(p.16)*.
- ☑ The nationalities from the different provinces wanted to be independent from Russian rule.

 What were the immediate causes of the February Revolution?

There were 6 key immediate causes of the February Revolution:

- ☑ The First World War caused significant disruption to Russia's economy and eroded the support for Nicholas II from the peasants, the working class, the middle class and the upper class.
- ☑ Russia was suffering from food and fuel shortages during the winter of 1916-17.

- By January 1917, the morale of the Russian Army was very low with 1.5 million deserting in 1916.
- On 9th February, there were massive strikes in Moscow and Petrograd.
- The strikes increased when, on 19th January, the Petrograd authorities announced bread would be rationed from 1st March.
- There was a huge march in Petrograd on 23rd February, celebrating International Women's Day, which became an anti-government protest against the war and the tsar.

What were the key events of the February Revolution?

There were 6 key events during the February Revolution:

- By 25th February, 200,000 people were on strike in Petrograd.
- On 26th February, Nicholas II ordered the fourth Duma to close down but they refused.
- On 27th February, Nicholas II ordered the army to shoot the protesters. 66,000 soldiers from the Petrograd garrison refused and mutinied, and joined the protesters instead. The Petrograd Soviet (p.66), or workers council, was created.
- On 28th February, the Petrograd Soviet (p.66) issued Order Number 1 which stated that the armed forces should only obey the orders of the Soviet. On the same day the sailors in Kronstadt mutinied. At this point, Nicholas II was asked to abdicate.
- On 1st March, the Soviets recognised the authority of the Provisional Government (p.61) set up by the fourth Duma under the leadership of Prince Lvov.
- Tsar Nicholas II abdicated on behalf of himself and his son on 2nd March, 1917.

What were the results of the February Revolution?

There were 3 main results of the February Revolution.

- The end of 300 years of Romanov rule and the end of the monarchy.
- This was followed by the end of the empire and the formation of the republic in the spring of 1917.
- The establishment of dual power (p.16), or dual authority, between the Russian Provisional Government (p.61) and the Petrograd Soviet (p.66) of Workers' and Soldiers' Deputies.

Why did the February Revolution succeed?

There were 6 main reasons the February Revolution succeeded:

- The main reason was the army failed to support Tsar Nicholas II and refused to fire on the protesters. The mutiny meant Nicholas II could no longer rely on the support of the army to prop up his government.
- Aristocrats and key members of his own government lost faith in Nicholas II, withdrew their support, and persuaded Nicholas II to abdicate.
- There was an alternative government to Nicholas II when the fourth Duma created the Provisional Government (p.61), which was supported by the Petrograd Soviet (p.66).
- Nicholas II was blamed for Russia's failures in the First World War and, as a result, he lost the support of many different social classes including the workers, the middle class and the aristocrats. He was left with little support.
- The shortages caused by the First World War significantly increased the amount of discontent in Russia, so opposition became much more widespread and more dangerous to Nicholas II's position.
- The reputation of the tsar's government had been fundamentally weakened by the failures in the First World War and the influence Rasputin was reputed to have had over Tsarina Alexandra.

How did the February Revolution affect the First World War?

The most significant mutiny of the war was that of the Russian armies on the Eastern Front during 1917. This was significant for 4 reasons:

- This mutiny was enabled by low morale and a loss of faith in tsarism.
- The mutiny helped the February revolution succeed. The Imperial Guard in Petrograd deserted and joined the revolution, signaling that both officers and men were not willing to defend the tsar.

- ☑ The February Revolution did not end the war on the Eastern Front. Despite many problems, the Provisional Government *(p.61)* remained loyal to the Triple Entente *(p.24)*.
- ☑ The Russian Army was still capable of fighting and this is shown in the June Offensive *(p.63)* of 1917.

DID YOU KNOW?

The February Revolution is often described as being 'spontaneous' in the sense that there was not one group that organised it.

THE PROVISIONAL GOVERNMENT

The Provisional Government lost the support of the people because it made several important mistakes.

What was the Provisional Government?

The Provisional Government was the temporary government set up in Russia after Tsar Nicholas II abdicated and the tsarist government collapsed.

When was the Provisional Government created?

The Provisional Government was created on 2nd March, 1917.

Who set up the Provisional Government?

The Provisional Government was created by 12 members of the fourth Duma. The initial leader was Prince Lvov, a liberal.

Who were the members of the Provisional Government?

The Provisional Government:

- ☑ Consisted of 12 members of the fourth Duma.
- ☑ Was led by Prince Lvov, a liberal, from March until July.
- ☑ Was led by Alexander Kerensky, a Socialist Revolutionary, from July until October.
- ☑ The other members were a mixture of Kadets and Octobrists.

What were the weaknesses of the Provisional Government?

The Provisional Government (PG) had 4 key weaknesses:

- ☑ It lacked authority because it shared power *(p.16)* with the Petrograd Soviet *(p.66)*.
- ☑ It lacked legitimacy because it didn't represent the people. It was made up of mainly upper class men and was not elected by the population.
- ☑ It lacked power *(p.16)* because the Petrograd Soviet's *(p.66)* Order Number One gave the Soviet control of the armed forces.
- ☑ It was not responsible for all areas of government because the Petrograd Soviet *(p.66)* controlled some, such as the transport system and soldiers.

What were the key actions of the Provisional Government?

The Provisional Government took 3 key actions:

- On 3rd March 1917, it published its eight principles of government including complete political and religious amnesty which allowed political prisoners to be released from prison, freedom of speech, and the setting up of a Constituent Assembly.

- It published a set of decrees including an eight hour working day, minimum wage, the abolition of the death sentence and the confiscation of all Crown lands.

- It launched the June Offensive (p.63) which was unsuccessful and led to the loss of 400,000 men and mutinies. Kerensky, the Minister of War, was blamed and it led to more social unrest.

What mistakes did the Provisional Government make?

The Provisional Government made 5 key mistakes:

- It continued the war with Germany. It had little choice as the Allies threatened to cut off financial aid if Russia pulled out of the war.

- It did not successfully deal with the issue of shortages of food and goods. Its economic measures, such as an increase in income tax, were just ignored.

- It did not address the needs of the peasants. They wanted more land from the landlords but the Provisional Government did nothing because, in reality, it had little control (p.16) over most of Russia and it would cost too much money.

- The Provisional Government introduced decrees which increased people's rights, including the ability to criticise its actions.

- It did not arrange elections, which made it seem the Provisional Government wanted to keep its power (p.16).

What difference did the Provisional Government make to the course of the First World War in Russia?

The Provisional Government did little to address the military problems on the Eastern Front. This was significant to the outcome of the war on the Eastern Front for 2 main reasons:

- The June Offensive (p.63) ended the ability of the Russian Army to continue the fight. It destroyed what was left of the armies morale.

- The faith that many soldiers had in their new government to end the war was lost.

What are historians' opinions on the effectiveness of the Provisional Government rule Russia in 1917?

Historians debate how effectively the Provisional Government ruled Russia during its brief time in power (p.16).

How was the Provisional Government effective?

There were 4 main ways that the Provisional Government ruled Russia effectively:

- It appealed to the people through its liberal approach. Its key principles included freedom of speech, the release of political prisoners and the abolition of the death sentence.

- It passed decrees to improve working conditions including a minimum wage and an eight hour working day.

- It always intended to set up a Constituent Assembly which would provide democratic elections.

- They effectively dealt with the riots and uprisings during the July Days and the Kornilov revolt (p.65).

How was the Provisional Government ineffective?

There were 9 main ways the Provisional Government was ineffective in ruling Russia:

- It never really achieved full authority over the country because it had to share power (p.16) with the Petrograd Soviet (p.66).

- The Petrograd Soviet (p.66) had control (p.16) of the army due to Order Number One.

- It was unelected and didn't really represent the people as it was mainly made up of aristocrats.

- It was responsible for the disastrous June Offensive (p.63) where 400,000 men were lost.

- It failed to deal with the problems of hunger and had to bring in food rationing.

- ☑ It was reliant on the Petrograd Soviet *(p.66)* and the Bolsheviks to put down the Kornilov revolt *(p.65)*.

- ☑ It failed to deal with land distribution which was the main grievance for the Russian peasants.

- ☑ It failed to pull Russia out of the war, which meant it failed to solve many of the problems which caused the downfall of the tsar in the first place.

- ☑ The increase in support for the Bolsheviks demonstrates how unpopular the Provisional Government became. Their famous slogan, "Peace, Land, Bread", represented the key areas where the Provisional Government failed to deliver.

DID YOU KNOW?

The Provisional Government did not represent the ordinary people of Russia. It was dominated by people from the upper classes.

THE JUNE OFFENSIVE, 1917

The last desperate Russian offensive of the war.

What was the June Offensive?

The June Offensive was a Russian attack to push back the Austro-Hungarians and Germans to win the war. It was a disaster. It is also known as the July Offensive depending on which calendar you are using.

When did the June Offensive take place?

The June Offensive began on 18th June, 1917 and had collapsed by 5th July, 1917 by the old calendar. By the new calendar it began on 1st July, 1917.

Why did the June Offensive occur?

The June Offensive was launched as an attempt by Russia to achieve a crushing military victory and end the war.

Who organised the June Offensive?

As the Minister for War, it was Alexander Kerensky who organised the June Offensive.

What were the results of the June Offensive?

There were 3 key results of the June Offensive:

- ☑ Huge losses of 400,000 men. It also led to mutinies and chaos.

- ☑ Both the Provisional Government *(p.61)* and Kerensky, as the minister of war, were blamed for the failures in the war. This led to resignations, especially from the Kadets.

- ☑ The July Days were a period of social, economic and political upheaval in Russia while the Provisional Government *(p.61)* was in charge.

DID YOU KNOW?

Lenin was an agent of the Germans. He was in exile in Switzerland but in April 1917 the German General Staff arranged for him to travel across Europe in a secret train back to Petrograd.

THE RUSSIAN JULY DAYS, 1917

A unplanned uprising.

What were the July Days in Russia?

The July Days were a period of social, economic and political upheaval in Russia while the Provisional Government *(p.61)* was in power *(p.16)*.

When were the July Days in Russia?

The July Days happened between 3rd and 7th July, 1917.

Why did the July Days happen in Russia?

There were 3 key reasons for the July Days uprising:

- ☑ Bread rationing was brought in by the Provisional Government *(p.61)* due to shortages in March 1917. By July these food shortages had worsened.
- ☑ The June Offensive *(p.63)* had totally failed and people were war weary.
- ☑ The Bolsheviks, under Lenin, had very successful anti-Provisional Government *(p.61)* propaganda.

What happened during the July Days in Russia?

There were 6 key events during the July Days uprising:

- ☑ Workers, soldiers and Kronstadt sailors protested in Petrograd.
- ☑ The Bolshevik Party organised riots. The crowds used the Bolshevik slogans of 'Peace, Bread and Land', and 'All Power *(p.16)* to the Soviets'.
- ☑ The Petrograd Soviet *(p.66)* rejected a demand for them to take control *(p.16)*.
- ☑ The Provisional Government *(p.61)*, with the help of loyal troops, cleared the streets and regained control *(p.16)*.
- ☑ Bolshevik leaders, including Trotsky, were rounded up and 800 members were arrested and imprisoned.
- ☑ Lenin fled to Finland and the reputation of the Bolsheviks was in tatters.

Who was involved with the July Days In Russia?

The protests during the July Days involved the following groups: revolutionaries, sailors, soldiers, Bolsheviks and workers.

What were the results of the July Days in Russia?

There were 3 key results of the July Days:

- ☑ The Provisional Government's *(p.61)* reputation was restored.
- ☑ The opponents of the Provisional Government *(p.61)* were imprisoned or had fled abroad, e.g. Lenin.
- ☑ Kerensky became the leader of the Provisional Government *(p.61)* and worked with the Kadets and Socialists.

How did the July Days affect the course of the First World War in Russia?

The July Days were significant on the outcome of the war on the Eastern Front for 3 reasons:

- ☑ This period proved that the Bolsheviks were now the group that spoke for the regular soldiers and sailors.
- ☑ Up to now the soldiers with the most political influence had been those in Petrograd. However, Bolshevik propaganda and Marxist ideas were becoming more prevalent with the troops at the front.
- ☑ Desertions from the front were increasing as experienced troops had been replaced with peasant conscripts with low morale.

THE KORNILOV REVOLT, 1917

General Kornilov was appointed to restore discipline in the army, yet led a revolt by the army.

What was the Kornilov Revolt?

The Kornilov Revolt, or the Kornilov Coup, was an unsuccessful coup by part of the army against the Russian Provisional Government *(p.61)* and the Petrograd Soviet *(p.66)*.

Who was the leader of the Kornilov Revolt?

General Lavr Kornilov was Commander-in-Chief of the Russian Army from July to September 1917. He was the leader of the Kornilov Revolt.

When was the Kornilov Revolt?

It happened from 27th to 30th August, 1917, using the old calendar. (In the new calendar, 10th to 13th September, 1917).

Why did the Kornilov Revolt happen?

There are 2 main reasons why the Kornilov Revolt occurred:

- Prime Minister Kerensky aimed to improve army discipline so that Russia could win the First World War. He appointed General Kornilov as the commander-in-chief of the army to bring about this change.
- General Kornilov wanted Kerensky to declare martial law and close down the soviets. Kerensky refused and sacked Kornilov who reacted by sending troops to Petrograd.

What happened during the Kornilov Revolt?

There were 4 key events during the Kornilov Revolt:

- On 24th August, General Kornilov ordered troops to Petrograd to close down the Petrograd Soviet *(p.66)*.
- Kerensky called on the Petrograd Soviet *(p.66)* to defend the city and allowed them to arm the Red Guard and in return he freed the Bolshevik prisoners arrested in the July Days uprising.
- General Kornilov's route into the city was blocked by railway workers.
- The Bolsheviks stopped General Kornilov and he was arrested on 1st September, 1917.

What were the results of the Kornilov Revolt?

The Kornilov Revolt affected the government and had 5 other important consequences:

- It weakened the position of the Provisional Government *(p.61)*. They lost support from the right-wing because they had given weapons to the Bolsheviks. They lost support from the left-wing because Kerensky had tried to compromise with Kornilov at first.
- The Bolsheviks had more support because they had defended Petrograd from General Kornilov and now they had weapons.
- Membership of the Bolshevik Party increased by about 100,000 by October.

☑ Because their position was strengthened, the Bolsheviks were able to gain control *(p.16)* of the Petrograd Soviet *(p.66)* by September 1917.

☑ Morale and discipline in the army decreased even more.

DID YOU KNOW?

General Kornilov was appointed commander-in-chief of the Russian Army in July 1917. According to him, he considered the Petrograd Soviet as being responsible for the collapse of the Russian Army on the Eastern Front.

THE PETROGRAD SOVIET

The Petrograd Soviet played a very important role in the October Revolution.

What was the Petrograd Soviet?

The Petrograd Soviet was a council of workers' and soldiers' deputies in Russia.

When was the Petrograd Soviet formed?

The Petrograd Soviet was formed on 12th March, 1917.

Who was the founder of the Petrograd Soviet?

The Petrograd Soviet was formed by Leon Trotsky.

Who were the members of the Petrograd Soviet?

The leaders of the Soviet were a mix of radical socialists, Mensheviks and Social Revolutionaries but also a small number of Bolsheviks. The leadership included Trotsky and Kerensky, who was also a member of the Provisional Government *(p.61)*.

Why was the Petrograd Soviet created?

The Petrograd Soviet was set up because of the massive unrest in Petrograd. Tsar Nicholas II's government was collapsing and soldiers declared their support for the revolution.

Why was the Petrograd Soviet important?

The Petrograd Soviet was important for 4 key reasons:

☑ It shared power *(p.16)* with the Provisional Government *(p.61)*, called the dual authority or dual power, between March 1917 and October 1917.

☑ It issued Order Number 1 on 1st March which stated the armed forces should only obey the orders of the Soviet. It should not obey the Provisional Government *(p.61)* if orders from that organisation contradicted or undermined those of the Soviet.

☑ It organised the defence of Petrograd during the Kornilov Revolt *(p.65)* in August 1917, using the Red Guard after the Provisional Government *(p.61)* gave them weapons.

☑ Trotsky used the Petrograd Soviet to help plan the October Revolution *(p.68)*.

In what ways was the Petrograd Soviet's impact limited?

The Petrograd Soviet's impact was limited in 4 key ways:

- It was reluctant to take power *(p.16)* because there were so many problems in Russia which would be incredibly difficult to solve. They did not want to take responsibility for failing to solve these problems.
- The Mensheviks in the Petrograd Soviet believed in a socialist revolution but they did not think that Russia was ready for the revolution yet. Therefore, they wanted to fully industrialise first and have a phase where it was controlled by the bourgeoisie or upper class.
- The Petrograd Soviet was prepared to support the Provisional Government *(p.61)* because it represented the upper class and, by supporting it, the Petrograd Soviet appeared to not prioritise the needs of the workers.
- It did not want to weaken the Provisional Government *(p.61)* because they feared the tsar would regain power *(p.16)*.

What was the impact of the Petrograd Soviet on the First World War in Russia?

The Petrograd Soviet was significant in undermining the ability of the Russian Army to continue to fight the war. It spoke for the regular soldiers and sailors. They now had an alternative leadership to listen to and follow.

> **DID YOU KNOW?**
>
> Each socialist party was given 3 seats on the Petrograd Soviet's executive committee, called Ispolkom, to give the group a more intellectual steer. However, meetings were often very long and almost as disorderly as the public meetings.

THE GROWTH OF BOLSHEVIK SUPPORT

The key Bolshevik slogan was 'Peace, Land, Bread.'

What was the Bolshevik growth in support?

There was a growth in support for the Bolshevik Party between February and October 1917, during the period when the Provisional Government *(p.61)* was in charge of Russia.

When was the growth in support for the Bolsheviks?

The growth in support for the Bolsheviks was between February and October 1917. In particular, there was a spurt in their growth during the summer after the Kornilov Revolt *(p.65)*.

Who supported the Bolshevik Party that led to a growth in its support?

Many soldiers, sailors and workers supported the Bolshevik Party.

Why did the Bolsheviks see a growth in support?

There were 6 key reasons why support for the Bolsheviks grew:

- Lenin's influence was considerable. His personality and determination encouraged other Bolsheviks to follow his lead.
- Lenin's 'April Theses' promised key things to key groups. 'Peace, Land and Bread' appealed to soldiers, peasants and workers.
- People's desperation to end the First World War was a key factor in the growth of Bolshevik support.
- Bolshevik newspapers spread their propaganda messages.
- The Provisional Government *(p.61)* became more unpopular after the Kornilov Revolt *(p.65)* whereas the Bolsheviks became more popular as they were seen as the defenders of Petrograd.

The Bolsheviks were able to build the Red Guards, a private Bolshevik army, led by Leon Trotsky and arm them with the weapons given to them during the Kornilov Revolt *(p.65)*.

How was the growth in support for the Bolsheviks significant to the First World War in Russia?

The growth in support for the Bolsheviks was significant to the outcome on the Eastern Front for 3 reasons:

 Lenin had been funded and supported by the German government. They knew by sending him to Russia he could subvert the Russian government and win the war for Germany without them having to fight.

 The Germans stopped their offensives on the Eastern Front during 1917 to avoid provoking Russia. They ordered their soldiers to encourage Russian deserters to cross the lines.

 Powerful *(p.16)* Bolshevik propaganda such as 'Peace, Bread, Land' offered a way out of the war for the average Russian soldier.

DID YOU KNOW?

Lenin returned to Russia in April 1917 with the help of the Germans.

THE OCTOBER REVOLUTION

The October Revolution was led by a small, dedicated group of revolutionaries.

What was the October Revolution?

The October Revolution is sometimes called the November Revolution due to Russia using a different calendar. It was the Bolshevik-led revolution to remove the Provisional Government *(p.61)* from power *(p.16)*.

When was the October Revolution?

The October Revolution occurred on 25th and 26th October, 1917, according to the old calendar. The dates are 7th and 8th November, 1917, under the new calendar.

Who led the October Revolution?

The October Revolution was organised by the Bolsheviks, led by Lenin. Leon Trotsky played a major role in organising the revolution.

Why did the October Revolution happen?

There were 5 key reasons why the October Revolution occurred:

 There was a shift in power *(p.16)* and popularity from the Provisional Government *(p.61)* to the Petrograd Soviet *(p.66)* after the Kornilov Revolt *(p.65)*.

 On 10th October, Lenin returned to Russia and was able to persuade leading Bolsheviks that the party should plan for an armed uprising against the Provisional Government *(p.61)*.

 On 16th October, Trotsky, as the leader of the Petrograd Soviet *(p.66)*, created the Military Revolutionary Committee. This gained the support of the Peter and Paul Fortress, so the Bolsheviks had the support of the military.

 On 24th October, the leader of the Provisional Government *(p.61)*, Kerensky, attempted to limit the power *(p.16)* of the Bolsheviks by ordering their arrest and stopping their newspapers. Trotsky used the Military Revolutionary Committee to take over key bridges and the telephone exchange.

 Lenin needed to act before the elections to the Constituent Assembly which were scheduled for November 1917.

What happened during the October Revolution?

There were 3 key events during the actual takeover:

- ☑ Early in the morning of 24th-25th October, the Red Guards took control *(p.16)* of banks, government buildings and the railway stations.
- ☑ In the evening of 25th October, the Red Guards entered the Winter Palace and arrested the members of the Provisional Government *(p.61)* that were present.
- ☑ On 26th October, Lenin announced a new communist government called the Council of the People's Commissars.

Why were the Bolsheviks successful during the October Revolution?

There were 5 key reasons why the Bolsheviks were successful during the October Revolution:

- ☑ Trotsky played a key role in the success of the October Revolution. He cleverly used his position as the elected leader of the Petrograd Soviet *(p.66)*, created the Military Revolutionary Committee, and helped increase support for the Bolsheviks.
- ☑ The Provisional Government *(p.61)* was weak because it had lost support from all parts of society. The armed forces were crumbling because of the First World War. The peasants felt neglected as their issues had not been addressed.
- ☑ Lenin's 'April Theses' appealed to the people, was clear to understand and helped to persuade other leading Bolsheviks not to support the Provisional Government *(p.61)*. His planning of the uprising was successful.
- ☑ They were funded by Germany which helped pay for their propaganda. The Germans hoped that the revolution would be successful so that Russia would pull out of the First World War.
- ☑ The Bolsheviks had the support of the major industrial cities.

What was the significance of the October Revolution to the First World War in Russia?

The October Revolution was significant to the outcome of the war on the Eastern Front for 4 reasons:

- ☑ Lenin had become popular on the slogan, 'Peace, Bread, Land' that reflected both the requirements of the German government and his need to stay in power *(p.16)* by delivering on his promise.
- ☑ The October revolution led directly to an armistice and the offer of Peace from the Bolsheviks.
- ☑ The negotiations stalled as the Bolsheviks tried to delay agreeing to the German and Austrian demands which were shocking to most Russians.
- ☑ The Germans resumed the war by launching a full scale assault against Petrograd, getting to within 100 miles of the Russian capital.

DID YOU KNOW?

The revolution started the break up of the Russian Empire. The Ukraine declared its independence in November 1917 and Finland declared its independence on the 6th December, 1917.

THE BOLSHEVIK CONSOLIDATION OF POWER

Bolsheviks had very little control over most of Russia after the October Revolution 1917. They had to expand control to all parts of the country.

What was the Bolshevik consolidation of power?

The Bolshevik consolidation of power was a period of time in which the Bolsheviks increased their control *(p.16)* from just Moscow and Petrograd to most of Russia.

When did the Bolshevik consolidation of power happen?

The Bolshevik consolidation of power was between 1917 and 1921.

How did the Bolsheviks consolidate their growth in power?

There were 6 main actions that the Bolsheviks took to consolidate their power *(p. 16)*:

- ☑ They issued several decrees between October and December 1917, including the Decree On Peace, the Decree on Land, the Decree on Nationalities and the Decree on Workers' Rights.
- ☑ The Bolsheviks shut down the Constituent Assembly in January 1918.
- ☑ In March 1918, they signed the Treaty of Brest-Litovsk *(p.71)* which ended the war with Germany.
- ☑ They fought and won the civil war against the Whites and the Greens between 1918 and 1921.
- ☑ They began the Red Terror by rounding up and executing thousands of their opponents.
- ☑ They brought in censorship and by 1921 had closed down all other political parties.

How did the Decree on Land help with the consolidation of the Bolsheviks' power?

The Bolsheviks issued the Decree on Land in October 1917, which abolished private ownership, including land owned by the tsar, the Church and private landowners. It was given to the peasants in the hope they would support the Bolsheviks.

How did the Decree on Peace help with the consolidation of Bolshevik power?

The Decree on Peace of October 1917, called for peace to be negotiated between all countries at war. Pulling Russia out of the war would mean the Bolsheviks could concentrate on establishing a government and consolidating their power *(p. 16)*.

How did the Decrees on Workers' Rights help with the consolidation of Bolshevik power?

The Decrees on Workers' Rights, issued in November 1917, focused on improvements to working conditions such as pay and unemployment benefits, and put the factories under the control *(p. 16)* of the workers in the hope the workers would support them.

How did the Decree on Nationalities help with the consolidation of the Bolsheviks' growth in power?

The Decree on Nationalities issued in October 1917, stated that the different nationalities could govern themselves. This was issued in the hope that they would not use the collapse of the tsarist government to gain their independence.

How did closing the Constituent Assembly help with the consolidation of Bolshevik power?

By closing down the Constituent Assembly on 6th January, 1918, Lenin prevented it being a source of opposition to the Bolsheviks. He was able to ban all political parties.

How did the consolidation of Bolshevik power affect the course of the First World War in Russia?

The period of Bolshevik consolidation from 1917-1921 had a significant effect on the outcome of the First World War for 5 main reasons:

- ☑ Lenin had time to crush the 'White' opposition in Russia and turn the former tsarist army into a revolutionary 'Red' army. This army would fight Russia's former allies during the Russian Civil War *(p. 73)*, 1918-1921.
- ☑ The Allies had now lost their most important ally, Russia. They offered to support the Bolshevik government if they committed to preserving the Triple Entente *(p.24)*, and continuing the war.
- ☑ Germany had proven that by supporting subversive groups you could win a war by destroying the home front.
- ☑ Events would backfire on Germany. Returning German prisoners of war brought back radical ideas of socialism and Marxism. It would take less than a year for these ideas to start the German revolution *(p.87)* that would depose the kaiser.

☑ When the Russian revolution began, all of Russia's former allies sent troops to support the 'Whites.' An argument can be made that the First World War did not end in 1919 with the Treaty of Versailles, but in 1921 with the end of the Russian Civil War *(p. 73)*.

DID YOU KNOW?

The following countries all sent troops to Russia to fight against the Bolsheviks: Britain, France, Japan, the USA, Italy, China, Poland, India, Canada, Australia, New Zealand, South Africa, Greece, Serbia, Romania, Estonia and Czechoslovakia.

THE RUSSIAN DEFEAT

'Situation serious. There is anarchy in the capital.' Mikhail Rodzianko, February 1917.

What was the Russian surrender in 1917?

In October 1917, Bolsheviks (communists) took control *(p. 16)* of Russia in a revolution. Their leader, Lenin, pulled Russia out of the First World War. An armistice was agreed in December and a peace treaty was signed in March 1918.

What was the impact of the Russian surrender on the First World War?

There were 3 main consequences of the Russian surrender:

☑ It ended the Triple Entente *(p. 24)*, weakening the Allied war effort.

☑ It allowed the Germans to transfer hundreds of thousands of troops to the Western Front and launch the Ludendorff Offensive *(p. 84)* in spring 1918.

☑ The peace treaty of Brest-Litovsk *(p. 71)* gave Germany vast areas of farmland and raw materials which helped in dealing with shortages caused by the Allied naval blockade.

DID YOU KNOW?

Russia suffered up to 2,750,000 dead during the First World War, contributing to the loss of faith in the tsar's leadership.

THE TREATY OF BREST LITOVSK, 1918

Lenin described the Treaty of Brest-Litovsk as, "that abyss of defeat, dismemberment, enslavement and humiliation."

What was the Brest-Litovsk Peace Treaty?

The Treaty of Brest-Litovsk ended Russia's role in the First World War. The treaty was signed at German-controlled Brest-Litovsk after two months of negotiations.

When was the Brest-Litovsk treaty signed?

The Treaty of Brest-Litovsk was signed on 3rd March, 1918.

Who signed the Brest-Litovsk Treaty?

The treaty was between the new Bolshevik government of Russia and the Central Powers - the German Empire, Austria-Hungary, Bulgaria and the Ottoman Empire.

Where was the Brest-Litovsk Treaty signed?

The Treaty of Brest-Litovsk was signed at the German Army's headquarters in Brest-Litovsk, which at that time was part of Poland. It is in modern Belarus.

Why did the Bolsheviks agree to sign the Brest-Litovsk Treaty?

There were 6 main reasons why the Bolsheviks agreed to sign the treaty:

- ✅ They had staked everything, and won all their support, on the promise of immediate withdrawal from the war.
- ✅ The Bolsheviks agreed to sign because they needed a swift end to war; Russia was not able to defeat Germany.
- ✅ If Russia lost the war, it would mean the end of the Bolshevik revolution.
- ✅ They believed Germany and the rest of Europe would also have communist revolutions, which would result in the treaty being overturned.
- ✅ Their priority was dealing with opposition to the Bolshevik revolution inside Russia, and they feared a civil war would begin.
- ✅ They could not afford to fight Germany and a civil war at the same time.

What was the outcome of the Brest-Litovsk Treaty?

There were 3 main terms of the treaty.

- ✅ Russia lost Finland, Estonia, Latvia, Lithuania, Ukraine, Georgia, and parts of Poland from its empire - this was more than a quarter of its farmland and railroads.
- ✅ It lost 26% of its population, or 62 million people.
- ✅ Germany imposed reparations, or compensation, of 300 million roubles.

What was the impact of the Treaty of Brest-Litovsk on Russia and the Bolshevik Party?

There were 4 main effects of the Treaty of Brest-Litovsk on Russia and the Bolshevik Party:

- ✅ It was considered a humiliation so people were furious with the Bolshevik Party for signing it.
- ✅ The land that Russia lost to Germany was some of the best farmland it had, so food shortages worsened.
- ✅ This led to mass migration of people from the towns and cities to the countryside in the search for food.
- ✅ Many right-wing people and tsarists were so horrified by the treaty that they were even more determined to oppose the Bolsheviks. This led to the civil war.

DID YOU KNOW?

Lenin was hoping that communist revolution would spread across Europe leading to the end of the First World War. He instructed the Russian delegates to make the peace negotiations with the Germans last longer. It wasn't until the Germans restarted the fighting on the Eastern Front, that the Russians signed the Treaty.

THE RUSSIAN CIVIL WAR, 1918-1921

The Bolsheviks winning the Russian Civil War centralised their control of the country and their own party.

What was the Russian Civil War?

A civil war was triggered by opposition to the Bolsheviks from various groups, including monarchists who wanted the tsar back in power *(p.16)*, anti-communists, groups angered by Brest-Litovsk and different nationalities who wanted their independence.

When was the Russian Civil War?

The Russian Civil War took place from 1918 to 1921.

Who fought in the Russian Civil War?

The Russian Civil War was fought between communist (Red) and anti-communist (White) forces. In addition, a number of countries, including Britain and the USA, sent troops to support the Whites. The Reds won.

What were the different armies involved in the Russian Civil War?

There were 3 main groups involved:

- ✅ The Red Army, who were the Bolsheviks or communists.
- ✅ The White Army, made up of nationalists and monarchists.
- ✅ The Green Army was formed by the peasants.

What were the causes of the Russian Civil War?

There were 5 key reasons why the Russian Civil War happened:

- ✅ The Russian Empire had collapsed because many nationalities wanted independence and the Bolshevik Decree on Nationalities allowed this. People who were pro-Empire wanted to re-conquer these areas.
- ✅ Political opposition had grown towards the Bolsheviks from the Social Revolutionaries, the Mensheviks, the Constituent Assembly, and the anti-Bolshevik alliance to form the Whites. People objected to the fact the Bolsheviks had seized power *(p.16)* undemocratically.
- ✅ The Allies were opposed to the Bolsheviks pulling out of the First World War and the signing of the Treaty of Brest-Litovsk *(p.71)*. They hoped that by supporting the Whites, the Bolsheviks would be defeated and Russia would re-enter the war.
- ✅ Law and order had broken down.
- ✅ Food requisitioning by the Bolsheviks angered the peasants and so they formed the Green Army to defend their homes.

What were the consequences of the Russian Civil War on international relations?

The Russian Civil War had 3 main consequences for international relations:

- ✅ It increased the Soviet Union's suspicion that the capitalist West would always seek to overthrow communism.
- ✅ In order to protect the USSR from future foreign interference, Lenin, the leader of the USSR, pursued a policy of worldwide communist revolution.
- ✅ This in turn caused a 'Red Scare' in 1920s America as many feared the worldwide spread of communism.

Who fought against the Bolsheviks in the Russian Civil War?

There were 3 main groups that opposed the Bolsheviks:

- ✅ The Whites consisted of lots of different groups such as Socialist Revolutionaries, tsarists/monarchists, Liberals, ultra-conservatives, and army officers against the Treaty of Brest-Litovsk *(p.71)*.

- ☑ The Greens consisted of peasants and deserters from other armies.
- ☑ Foreign countries also intervened in the civil war against the Bolsheviks. Britain, Japan and USA all interfered.

What were the key events of the Russian Civil war?

There were 9 key events during the Russian Civil War:

- ☑ Trotsky became the Commissar for War for the Bolsheviks and took charge of the Red Army on 13th March, 1918.
- ☑ In May 1918, the Czech Legion rebelled against the Red Army. They were leaving Russia when Trotsky demanded their weapons. They responded by allying with the Socialist Revolutionaries and taking over parts of the Trans-Siberian Railway.
- ☑ On 17th July, 1918, Tsar Nicholas II and his family were executed in Yekaterinburg to prevent the Whites and the Czech Legion from rescuing them and using them as a rallying point in the Civil War.
- ☑ In August 1918, Trotsky increased the harsh discipline in the Red Army so that one in every ten soldiers was shot if he retreated.
- ☑ The Bolsheviks suffered a major set-back during the Eastern Front Offensive led by one of the White's leaders, Admiral Kolchak. He attacked in June 1918. However, the Red Army managed to force the Whites to retreat by June 1919.
- ☑ By October 1919, the Red Army had managed to stop General Yudenich's advance on Petrograd and General Denikin's advance on Moscow.
- ☑ Between April and October 1920, the Bolsheviks were also at war with Poland until they signed the Treaty of Riga in October.
- ☑ The Whites were finally defeated at the Battle of Perekop between 7th and 15th November, 1920.
- ☑ In 1921, the Green Army, led by General Makhno, was finally defeated in the Ukraine and by General Antonov in Tambov where about 50,000 peasants had led an uprising against the Bolsheviks.

Why did the Bolsheviks win the Russian Civil War?

There are 6 main reasons why the Bolsheviks won:

- ☑ The Bolsheviks had control (p.16) of the industrial heartlands and transport links, which gave them a great advantage over their enemies. They had control over factories which made munitions.
- ☑ The Bolsheviks had a strong, well-organised propaganda machine and used art, posters and entertainment to spread their message.
- ☑ They introduced conscription into the Red Army so they had five million soldiers by 1921.
- ☑ As commissar for war, Trotsky introduced harsh military discipline, recruited tsarist officers for their experience and used the agitprop trains to spread propaganda. He turned the Red Army into an effective force and his harsh discipline ensured loyalty to the Reds.
- ☑ The Red Terror undermined opposition to the Bolsheviks as the Cheka, or secret police, executed 50,000 of their enemies in 1918 including the tsar and his family.
- ☑ Lenin's economic policy of War Communism took control (p.16) of food production and manufacturing, which ensured the army was supplied.

Why did the Whites lose the Russian Civil War?

There were 6 key reasons why the Whites lost the civil war:

- ☑ They were reliant on foreign assistance for supplies and money, so the Whites were portrayed as the invading army.
- ☑ There was a severe lack of planning because they did not have one single leader as it was not a unified group.
- ☑ There were problems with communication, geographical distances and rivalry between the leaders.
- ☑ They were not united by a single goal as some wanted a return to tsarism, others favoured a military dictatorship and others preferred the Constituent Assembly.
- ☑ The Whites did not control (p.16) the major areas of industry, population or transport links because they tended to be on the outer edges of Russia.
- ☑ As a result their army was smaller and not as well supplied.

What were the consequences of the Russian Civil War?

There were 5 main consequences of the civil war.

- ☑ The Bolsheviks consolidated *(p.69)* their control *(p.16)* over the country, economically with the policy of War Communism and politically as they destroyed their opposition using the Red Terror and by winning the civil war.
- ☑ The policy of War Communism left the country economically ruined as food production and manufacturing collapsed.
- ☑ There was unrest with strikes and several different peasant uprisings, including the Tambov Uprising from 1920 to 1921, and the Kronstadt Uprising in 1921.
- ☑ Around eight million people died.
- ☑ The leaders of the Bolshevik Party centralised control *(p.16)* over their party as well as the country. All decisions were made by seven to nine key members of the Politburo and orders were passed down to the rank and file.

> ### DID YOU KNOW?
>
> Power was centralised in the Politburo, the key decision-making body of the Communist Party.

THE ZIMMERMANN TELEGRAM, 1917

German bad luck and British cryptography

 ## What was the Zimmermann Telegram?

The Zimmermann Telegram was a secret diplomatic message that was discovered by the British. It helped to swing the American public into supporting a war against Germany.

 ## When was the Zimmermann Telegram sent?

The Zimmermann Telegram was sent on 16th January, 1917. It was given to the American government at the end of February and was reported in newspapers on 1st March, 1917.

 ## What did the Zimmermann Telegram say?

The telegram instructed the German ambassador to Mexico to suggest the following proposals to the Mexican government:

- ☑ It said that Germany would offer financial and military support to Mexico, if Mexico attacked the United States.
- ☑ It requested the Mexicans to ask Japan to become an ally of Germany.

 ## How was the Zimmermann Telegram discovered?

The telegram was discovered because the British had broken the German secret codes. This enabled them to decipher the message.

 ## Who sent the Zimmermann Telegram?

The Zimmermann Telegram involved several governments and people:

- ☑ The top secret telegram was sent by the German Foreign Secretary Arthur Zimmermann, to the German ambassador in Mexico.
- ☑ The British intelligence services intercepted and decoded the telegram.

☑ The British handed the telegram to the American government.

 What were the consequences of the Zimmermann Telegram?

There were 3 key consequences of the Zimmermann Telegram:

☑ In March, the contents of the telegram had been released to the world's press. The unfortunate Zimmermann admitted that he written the note. The world now had another reason to see Germany as a dangerous and aggressive nation.

☑ Public opinion in the United States began to turn in favour of war, especially as the Germans had recently resumed unrestricted submarine warfare *(p.49)*. This made many Americans angry.

☑ Woodrow Wilson now felt confident enough to ask Congress to declare war against Germany on 2nd April 1917.

DID YOU KNOW?

Cryptography is the art of writing or breaking coded messages. British Military Intelligence, Section 1, or MI1 was the government office responsible for trying to decypher coded enemy messages during the First World War.

THE US ENTRY TO THE WAR

Here come the Yankees!

 What did the USA do when it joined the First World War?

When the USA joined the First World War it reinforced the Allies in Europe, and helped by continuing to supply other allies with food, arms, money, and raw materials.

 When did the USA join the First World War?

The USA formally declared war in April 1917.

 Why did the USA enter the First World War?

The USA joined the First World War for two key reasons:

☑ The 'Zimmerman Telegram', from the German foreign secretary to the German ambassador in Mexico, was leaked in January 1917. It offered military and financial support if Mexico agreed to invade the USA. While the Mexicans did not agree, this created tension between Germany and the USA.

☑ Germany had restarted its unrestricted U-boat campaign. This resulted in the sinking of five American ships in March 1917. As the USA had warned Germany against this after the sinking of the Lusitania *(p.51)*, it felt it had no choice but to declare war on Germany.

 When did American troops arrive in Europe after they entered the First World War?

The first American troops landed in Europe in June 1917.

 How did America's entry into the First World War help the Allies?

America's entry into the First World War helped in 4 key ways:

☑ By May 1918 there were over one million US troops in France with tens of thousands arriving each week.

☑ They enlarged French ports so arriving ships could deliver more men and supplies.

☑ They built over 1,600km of railway lines to help continue the supply chain.

✅ They laid over 16,000km of telephone and telegraph cables, to help improve communications between lines.

 ## Why was US entry into the First World War important?

There were a number of significant events in which the USA was involved:

✅ In the Second Battle of the Marne *(p.31)*, two divisions of American soldiers helped to prevent German forces taking Paris during the Ludendorff Offensive *(p.84)*.

✅ In the Second Battle of Albert, in August 1918, 108,000 US soldiers helped capture 8,000 German soldiers.

✅ On 12th September 1918, in the Saint-Mihiel Offensive, 500,000 US soldiers attacked the salient created during the Ludendorff Offensive *(p.84)*. Within four days, the salient was under Allied control *(p.16)*.

✅ Between 26th September and 11th November 1918, the US led a combined US-Franco force of more than one million men. Using 300 tanks and 500 US aircraft *(p.39)*, the force advanced 32km towards the German border.

✅ The US was able to supply the Allies with large numbers of tanks and artillery. *(p.42)*

DID YOU KNOW?

During the First World War, American soldiers were nicknamed 'doughboys' and over 10,000 American military nurses served overseas in places such as France, Russia, Italy, China, Britain and Belgium.

THE BRITISH HOME FRONT

Canaries and the Land Army.

 ## What was the home front like in Britain in the First World War?

The First World War was the first war to have such a significant impact on the lives of civilians and non-combatants in Britain.

 ## How did the law change on the home front in Britain in the First World War?

In 1914, the British government passed the Defence of the Realm Act *(p.78)*, otherwise known as DORA. This gave it widespread and far-reaching powers to control *(p.16)* the behaviour of the public in order to protect the war effort.

 ## What was the effect of conscription on the home front in Britain in the First World War?

As the war progressed, Britain introduced more measures to ensure that a sufficient number of men joined the army:

✅ For the first two years of the war, Britain relied on volunteers, and approximately 3 million men had been recruited by 1916.

✅ Because of the number of casualties on the Western Front, conscription was introduced for single men aged between 18 and 41 in January 1916.

✅ In May 1916, conscription was extended to include married men aged between 18 and 41.

 ## How was food affected on the home front in Britain in the First World War?

Britain was vulnerable to food shortages because it imported most of its food. The German U-boat blockade had 4 serious consequences:

✅ Imports of food from the USA were increased.

✅ The government attempted to keep the price of bread at 9d a loaf, and wealthier people were discouraged from buying it, as it was a staple food for the poor.

Get our free app at GCSEHistory.com

77

- ☑ The amount of farmland was increased. Parks were requisitioned for the growing of food.
- ☑ Rationing was introduced for sugar and meat in January 1918, with other products rationed later in the year.

How were women on the home front in Britain in the First World War affected?

The war affected women in Britain in the following ways:

- ☑ The proportion of women in the workforce rose, from 24% in 1914 to 37% in 1918.
- ☑ Women took on new roles, in munitions factories, engineering and transport.
- ☑ When men returned from the war, most women were forced out of work into their pre-war positions.
- ☑ Women in Britain were granted the vote in 1918, ostensibly as a reward for their war work.

How many people were killed on the home front in Britain in the First World War?

The dangers of life in war-time meant that many civilians lost their lives.

- ☑ 16,829 civilians from Britain and her empire were killed as a result of enemy action during the war.
- ☑ Nearly a million civilians across the world are estimated to have been killed by fighting during the First World War.
- ☑ 5.9 million civilians across the world are thought to have died of disease, malnutrition and accidents as a direct result of the First World War.
- ☑ A pandemic of Spanish flu at the end of the war may have killed up to 50 million people globally.

DID YOU KNOW?

Female munitions workers were nicknamed 'canaries' after a small yellow bird. This was due to their skin being stained yellow by the TNT (explosives) that they filled the artillery shells with.

THE DEFENCE OF THE REALM ACT

New powers to control the public.

? What was the Defence of the Realm Act?

The Defence of the Realm Act (DORA) was a law passed in Britain shortly after the outbreak of the First World War in August 1914. It gave the government new powers to control *(p.16)* the public in the interests of the war effort.

What did the Defence of the Realm Act do?

DORA's powers were designed to protect 'public safety' during the war. They included:

- ☑ Press censorship.
- ☑ Reduced licensing hours, to limit how much time workers could spend drinking in pubs.
- ☑ The introduction of British Summer Time.
- ☑ Imprisonment without trial.
- ☑ The requisition of land and buildings for the war effort.
- ☑ Restrictions on the behaviour of individuals, including a ban on buying binoculars, flying kites or feeding bread to pigeons.
- ☑ Government control *(p.16)* over mines and railways.

What were the aims of the Defence of the Realm Act?

DORA aimed to protect the war effort and support Britain in winning the First World War. To do this, it tried to:

- ☑ Coordinate industry and agriculture to provide effectively for the troops at the front and the population at home.
- ☑ Prevent crucial information from falling into enemy hands.
- ☑ Keep morale high, to ensure that the British population continued to support the war effort.

What was the impact of the Defence of the Realm Act?

Approximately 260 regulations were introduced by DORA, and their effects were far-reaching:

- ☑ 90% of imports were eventually controlled by the government under DORA.
- ☑ Nearly a million people are estimated to have been arrested under DORA, and eleven were executed as spies.

DID YOU KNOW?

The British secret intelligence service, MI5, used the Boy Scouts and the Girl Guides to carry secret messages for them.

THE RUSSIAN HOME FRONT

'...the Russian Empire is run by lunatics...' Maurice Paleologue, French ambassador.

What were the effects of the First World War on Russia?

Russia suffered massive social, economic and political effects because of the First World War.

What were the economic effects of the First World War on Russia?

The First World War had 5 major economic effects on Russia:

- ☑ The transport system could not cope because it was so archaic. There were few railways or proper roads. The whole system broke down due to the demands of the mobilisation of the army, and transporting weapons, resources and food.
- ☑ The number of men conscripted into the armed forces meant there was a shortage of workers in the factories and on the farms. This led to shortages of goods and food.
- ☑ The national debt increased because the government had to borrow money, and taxes were increased to pay for the war.
- ☑ Russia lost resources when Germany occupied parts of the empire. The impact of this was worsened because Germany also cut off Russia's access to their allies, on whom they relied for imports. These supplies had to come via the port of Vladivostok, which was frozen in winter.
- ☑ The government printed too much paper money, which caused the Russian rouble to fall in value. This led to inflation.

What were the social effects of the First World War on Russia?

There were 4 key social effects of the First World War:

- ☑ Rural areas were stripped of men as they went to fight.
- ☑ There were food shortages because the transport system couldn't cope and food was requisitioned to feed the army.
- ☑ The shortages of goods and food, combined with the government printing more money, led to inflation of 200% by 1916. Working class people struggled as prices rose faster than wages.

☑ Unemployment rose in the cities. Demand for goods dropped, and factories could not get the resources they needed due to the collapse of the transport system.

 ## What were the political effects of the First World War on Russia?

There were 5 key political effects of the First World War:

☑ There was increased opposition to Nicholas II from the fourth Duma.

☑ Tsarina Alexandra was made regent when Nicholas II took charge of the army. Her incompetence led to an increase in opposition to the government.

☑ There was increased criticism of the tsarina because of Rasputin's influence over her and the decisions she made.

☑ Many historians argue that Nicholas II was greatly weakened by the First World War and that his mistakes, his increased unpopularity and his defeats were the main reasons he fell from power *(p.16)*.

☑ Others argue that Nicholas II would have fallen from power *(p.16)* without the First World War, due to the pre-existing social and economic problems, and the political opposition he already faced. The war simply sped things up.

 ## What were the effects of the First World War on the relationship between the tsar and the Duma in Russia?

The First World War ruined the relationship between Tsar Nicholas II and the fourth Duma in 4 key ways:

☑ Nicholas II initially suspended the fourth Duma against its wishes in August 1914.

☑ Members criticised Nicholas II's handling of the war and demanded the Duma had more of a say in how the country and the war was run. Nicholas II refused to make changes.

☑ In 1915, members of the fourth Duma created the Progressive Bloc, consisting of the centre parties. It tried to make the government, and Nicholas II, more responsive to the people. It failed.

☑ The fourth Duma was very critical of Tsarina Alexandra and Rasputin.

 ## What were the effects of the First World War on Tsarina Alexandra of Russia?

The First World War changed the position of Tsarina Alexandra in 4 main ways:

☑ When Nicholas II took command of the army in August 1915 he made Alexandra his regent. She was now in charge in his absence.

☑ Alexandra believed in autocracy. She would not work with the fourth Duma which, as a result, was very critical of her.

☑ She appointed ministers who were not always competent.

☑ She became highly criticised by the people because she was German, and because of her decisions as regent and her friendship with Rasputin.

DID YOU KNOW?

Russia had vasts amount of manpower and was able to mobilise approximately 15,800,000 men during the war.

80   *Quizzes, amazing exam preparation tools and more at GCSEHistory.com*

THE FRENCH HOME FRONT

'The strain on France has almost reached breaking point...' Erich von Falkenhayn, Chief of the German General Staff 1915

 What happened with France and the First World War?

The First World War had a huge impact on French politics, economy and society.

 How was France affected by the First World War?

France was negatively affected by the First World War in 6 key ways:

- ☑ The French economy suffered. 12% of France was occupied by Germany, which led to 300,000 houses and 20,000 shops or factories being destroyed.
- ☑ After the war the value of the French franc fell and investment dropped by 44%.
- ☑ The Germans had invaded France in the First World War and committed atrocities during their occupation. This motivated post-war French governments to focus on keeping Germany weak and signing treaties to keep France safe.
- ☑ French society was hit hard as the French suffered the highest casualty rate to men mobilised. About 11% of the population was killed or wounded. Birth rates fell after the war and there was a shortage of working-age men.
- ☑ Vast areas of French farmland had been fought over and were now dangerous wastelands full of live ammunition, and dead soldiers and animals.

 How did France become involved in the First World War?

The following events led to France entering the First World War.

- ☑ The Russians mobilised their army on the 31st July, 1914 despite the French government asking for caution. The French knew that this would cause German mobilisation, but Russia went ahead anyway.
- ☑ In response to Russian mobilisation, Germany declared war on Russia on the 1st August. It then put into motion the Schlieffen Plan *(p.26)*, which would begin the attack on Belgium and France.

 How was French society affected by the First World War?

French society was affected by the First World War in 7 key ways:

- ☑ 7.9 million French citizens served in the armed forces between 1914 and 1918.
- ☑ About 600,000 non-French citizens from the colonies served in the French army, with many seeing combat in France.
- ☑ About 4.2 million French soldiers were wounded, and over 500,000 were taken prisoner during the war.
- ☑ Nearly 1.4 million French soldiers were killed fighting in the First World War.
- ☑ Women had more opportunities to work as they had to take the place of men in the workplace.
- ☑ In 1917 there were widespread mutinies in the French army; 3,247 soldiers were put on trial and 49 were executed. However, French soldiers forced the government to improve their pay, living conditions and rights to visit their families.
- ☑ Rationing and the use of ration cards was introduced.

 How was the French economy affected by the First World War?

The First World War had 5 significant effects on the French economy:

- ☑ Prices for food increased by 25% at the start of 1917 causing shortages for the people of France.
- ☑ During the war, 1.7 million people worked producing armaments, including 420,000 women.
- ☑ The Colonial Labour Organization Service brought 200,000 colonial workers from the empire to work.
- ☑ Employment opportunities resulted in increased income for married working women.
- ☑ By the mid-1920s the French franc had fallen from its value of 20 cents against the dollar to an all-time low of 2 cents.

What were the political effects of the First World War on France?

The First World War had 7 significant effects on French politics:

☑ The French government had amassed huge loans to finance the war and had to repay them during the 1920s and 1930s.

☑ There were strikes throughout 1917, often led by women who wanted fairer levels of pay and conditions. They helped to organise unions to stand up for workers' rights.

☑ France had to ensure Germany paid reparations to help pay off its war debts.

☑ During the 1920s and 1930s, war debts forced France to keep a large standing army to help force Germany to stick to the Treaty of Versailles and to secure French borders.

☑ After the experience of high casualties, there was strong pressure for France to avoid future conflicts during the 1920s and 1930s.

☑ Inflation and the fall in living standards for the middle class helped cause political problems in France during the 1930s.

☑ After the war, French politics became very bitter and divided. The split between the left and right in France risked leading to civil war in the 1930s.

DID YOU KNOW?

Colonial workers came from the French empire to work on the French home front. This included people from French Indo-China (Vietnam, Laos and Cambodia), China and North Africa.

THE GERMAN HOME FRONT

The path to Hitler starts here.

 What happened with Germany and the First World War?

The First World War had a huge impact on Germany's society, politics and economy.

 How did Germany enter the First World War?

The following 3 key events led to Germany entering the First World War.

☑ Germany declared war on Russia on the 1st August, 1914.

☑ After Germany invaded France via Belgium, Great Britain declared war on Germany on the 4th August.

☑ This was followed by the Ottoman Empire (Turkey) joining the war a few months later, in October, where it supported Germany.

 How was Germany affected by the First World War?

Germany was affected in 3 key ways:

☑ Germany was economically damaged and the country's debt increased to 150 billion marks.

☑ They were affected socially with two million troops and approximately 763,000 civilians dead.

☑ They were affected politically with many groups attempting to seize power *(p. 16)*, the Kaiser's abdication and Germany becoming a republic.

How did the First World War affect people socially in Germany?

Germany was badly hit by the war because of the Allied Naval Blockade that stopped supplies getting into Germany during the war, and remained in place until the signing of the Treaty of Versailles, leaving many starving and ill.

 How many casualties did the First World War claim in Germany?

Germany was affected socially by the First World War in 5 key ways:

- ✅ They had a high casualty rate with approximately two million dead soldiers.
- ✅ Some 600,000 women were left as widows.
- ✅ The war also took its toll on civilians, with approximately 763,000 people dying from starvation.
- ✅ The gap between rich and poor had grown as a result of the war and increased social divisions.
- ✅ Over 1 and a half million soldiers returned home following the war, many struggling to adapt back to civilian life and accept defeat.

 What happened to Germany's economy after the First World War?

There were 7 significant negative effects on the economy:

- ✅ By 1918, industrial production was reduced by a third from 1913 levels.
- ✅ Fuel was short as a result of the war and consequently 300,000 people died from hypothermia.
- ✅ The government's budget was stretched by paying pensions to the 600,000 widows and 2 million orphans left after the war.
- ✅ Germany's debt was 50 billion German marks in 1914. This rapidly increased to 150 billion by 1918.
- ✅ Germany was bankrupt as it had spent all its gold reserves on the war.
- ✅ Inflation increased as a result of the weak German mark so the prices of goods were increasing.
- ✅ Germany was forced to begin interim payments to the Allies immediately after armistice was signed.

 What happened to Germany politically at the end of the First World War?

There were 5 important political effects:

- ✅ There was massive political unrest with uprisings and strikes, such as the naval mutiny in Kiel in October, 1918.
- ✅ The unrest spread to become the German Revolution *(p.87)* began, with huge consequences for the government and constitution of Germany.
- ✅ A communist state was declared in Bavaria on 7th November, 1918.
- ✅ The kaiser lost control *(p.16)* and abdicated.
- ✅ The new Weimar Republic was created, and by signing the Treaty of Versailles, was greatly resented by the German people.

 What were the events of the revolution in Germany before the end of the First World War?

There were 10 main events that occurred during the German Revolution *(p.87)*:

- ✅ The allies offered Germany an armistice to end the war. Part of their deal included that Germany become a democracy and the Kaiser should abdicate.
- ✅ The kaiser declined these terms, wishing to continue with the war.
- ✅ In response, the German Navy mutinied at the end of October 1918, refusing to follow the Kaiser's orders.
- ✅ Soon a domino effect occurred and by November 1918, there were demonstrations and strikes all across Germany and a communist state declared in Bavaria.
- ✅ On the advice of his government and the army, Kaiser Wilhelm abdicated on 9th November, 1918 and fled to the Netherlands.
- ✅ Philipp Scheidemann, a member of the Social Democratic Party (SPD), announced that Germany was a republic to prevent a communist government being declared on 9th November, 1918.

- Prince Max von Baden stepped down as the kaiser's chancellor. Friedrich Ebert, the leader of the SPD, took over as the chancellor of Germany.
- On 10th November, 1918, Ebert suspended the Reichstag (parliament) and formed the Council of People's Representatives to run the country until a new constitution was written.
- Germany signed a ceasefire or armistice with the Allies on 11th November, 1918 to end the fighting in the First World War.
- In January 1919, there were elections to the Constituent Assembly, or National Assembly, which would decide on the new constitution.

What were the consequences of the German Revolution before the end of the First World War?

There were 3 key results of the German revolution *(p.87)*:

- The kaiser abdicated.
- Germany became a republic.
- This led to the end of the First World War.

DID YOU KNOW?

The winter of 1916–1917 was known as the 'Turnip Winter' in Germany. Turnips were about the only food available to feed many people.

THE LUDENDORFF OFFENSIVE, 1918

Germany's last gamble.

What was the Ludendorff Offensive?

The Ludendorff Offensive, also known as the 1918 Spring Offensive or Kaiserschlacht, was a series of German attacks along the Western Front.

Why was the Ludendorff Offensive launched?

The offensive was launched by Germany for a number of reasons:

- The USA was sending 50,000 troops each month to the Western Front, along with vast amounts of weapons and equipment.
- The withdrawal of Russia freed up hundreds of thousands of troops from the Eastern Front.
- By 1918 the British naval blockade meant Germany was running out of food and war materials.

Who planned the Ludendorff Offensive?

Erich Ludendorff, a German general, planned the campaign.

When did the Ludendorff Offensive happen?

The offensive was launched on 21st March 1918 and ended in July 1918.

What happened during the Ludendorff Offensive?

The Ludendorff Offensive was a series of key events:

- On 21st March, 600 German guns began a five-hour bombardment of enemy trenches. This was followed by the release of mustard gas.
- Specially trained and lightly armed stormtroopers then advanced towards the enemy trenches, moving quickly and bypassing strong defences.
- As the British retreated, tens of thousands were captured and the Germans continued to advance.
- 100,000 German infantry soldiers then followed and this strategy allowing the Germans to capture 65km of French territory by July.
- At the Second Battle of the Marne *(p.31)*, 20,000 US troops arrived to reinforce the Allies. This halted the German attack.

Why did the Ludendorff Offensive fail?

The offensive failed for a number of reasons:

- Ludendorff sent too many men into France. He did not have any reserves or replacement troops.
- The offensive moved too quickly. The supply chain couldn't keep up and soldiers ran out of food and ammunition.
- The attack created a salient in the German line, which could be attacked from three sides. This meant the Germans were vulnerable to counter-attacks which could break their line.
- Hungry German soldiers stopped to loot food and wine from captured villages and Allied supply dumps, slowing the advance.

DID YOU KNOW?

The Germans built a supergun which they used to shell Paris. It could fire shells from 120 kms away. They called it the Kaiser Wilhelm Gun.

THE HUNDRED DAYS OFFENSIVE, 1918

Germany in retreat.

What was the 100 Days Offensive?

The 100 Days Offensive was a series of Allied attacks which ended the First World War.

What happened during the 100 Days Offensive?

There were 2 key events of the 100 Days Offensive:

- At Amiens an artillery *(p.42)* attack and creeping barrage broke through the German lines and allowed an Allied advance of 25km. Allied troops also captured 48,000 German soldiers.
- After breaking the front line at Amiens, the Allies forced the Germans back to the Hindenburg *(p.95)* Line which was broken by 8th October. At this point, the Germans were now in all-out retreat.

When was the 100 Days Offensive?

The offensive began with the Battle of Amiens on 8th August 1918, and ended officially on 11th November 1918 when Germany signed the Armistice.

Why was the 100 Days Offensive important?

The 100 Days Offensive was important for 2 key reasons:

- ☑ It allowed the Allies to break the Hindenburg *(p.95)* Line, a defensive line of three trench systems. Once this was broken, the Germans retreated in huge numbers.
- ☑ The offensive led to the German High Command seeking an armistice which came into effect on 11th November, 1918.

DID YOU KNOW?

During the 100 Days Offensive, it's estimated the Allies took 17,000 prisoners and 330 guns. Total German losses were estimated at 30,000 men, while around 6,500 Allied troops were killed, wounded or missing.

THE KIEL MUTINY

The proclamation of the German Republic.

What was the Kiel Mutiny?

The Kiel mutiny was a major revolt by sailors of the German High Seas Fleet.

When was the Kiel Mutiny?

The Kiel mutiny took place from the 28th October to the 4th November 1918.

Where did the Kiel Mutiny take place?

The mutiny took place at two locations. Wilhelmshaven where the High Seas Fleet was anchored and the Kiel naval base.

What were the causes of the Kiel Mutiny in the First World War?

There were 5 main reasons for the Kiel Mutiny in 1918:

- ☑ The morale of the sailors in the High Seas Fleet had fallen due to the fact they had been in port since the Battle of Jutland *(p.49)*.
- ☑ Socialist ideas had influenced many of the sailors who no longer trusted their officers.
- ☑ The High Seas Fleet was ordered on one last mission to take on the Royal Navy in the North Sea. This was in late October 1918 and it was clear the war was over.
- ☑ German officers looked forward to this last ditch suicide mission to save the kaiser's honour.
- ☑ Regular German sailors disagreed with this and revolted, taking control *(p.16)* of their ships and the Kiel naval yard.

What was the significance of the Kiel Mutiny?

The Kiel Mutiny was significant for 4 key reasons:

- ☑ The mutiny forced the navy to call off the final attack and the High Seas Fleet remained in Kiel.
- ☑ The sailors were quickly joined by workers from the city of Kiel and they quickly rounded up their officers and took control *(p.16)* of their battleships.
- ☑ The sailors formed sailors' and workers' councils similar to the soviets that appeared in Russia during the 1917 revolution.
- ☑ Within days the mutineers made demands for political freedom and their influence had spread across Germany, sparking the German Revolution *(p.87)* of 1918.

THE GERMAN REVOLUTION, 1918

The Breaking Point.

What was the German Revolution?

The German revolution was an uprising led by members of the navy, army and the workers who demanded peace negotiations to end the war in November 1918. This resulted in the collapse of the monarchy and the creation of a republic by January 1919.

What was the German Revolution also known as?

The German Revolution of 1918 is sometimes called 'the November Revolution'.

When was the German Revolution?

The German Revolution began after the Kiel Mutiny *(p.86)*, at the end of October 1918, with a new republic established in January 1919. It is often called 'the November Revolution' because most of the key events occurred in that month.

What caused the German Revolution?

The German revolution happened due to the economic problems of the war, war weariness and food shortages.

THE ARMISTICE, 1918

'...there is not one soldier in 50 that wants to go back to the front. They dread it.'
Australian war correspondent, Charles Bean.

What was the armistice at the end of the First World War?

The armistice was an agreement to end the First World War.

Who signed the armistice at the end of the First World War?

The armistice was signed by France, Britain, and Germany.

Where was the armistice at the end of the First World War signed?

The armistice that ended the First World War was signed in a railway carriage in Compiegne, France.

When was the armistice signed at the end of the First World War?

The armistice was signed at 5:12am on 11th November 1918, although it was agreed the ceasefire would begin at 11am on the 11th day of the 11th month.

What were the terms of the armistice at the end of the First World War?

There were 7 main terms agreed including:

- ☑ German troops were to leave France, Luxembourg, Belgium and Alsace-Lorraine within 14 days.
- ☑ Once they had left these territories, German troops were then to leave the territory on the west side of the Rhine.
- ☑ The treaties that Germany had forced on Russia and Romania would be cancelled.
- ☑ The German fleet would be taken away.
- ☑ Germany was to give up all its submarines, 5,000 cannons, 25,000 machine guns, 1,700 planes, 5,000 locomotive engines and 150,000 railcars.
- ☑ All British, French and Italian prisoners of war were to be freed after a peace treaty had been agreed upon.
- ☑ Germany would be blamed for the war and pay reparations for the damage that resulted from the war.

Why was the armistice agreed at the end of the First World War?

There were 3 main reasons why the armistice was agreed including:

- ☑ The First World War dragged on far longer than expected. It caused huge damage to both sides. Millions of soldiers and civilians were killed, along with the destruction of houses, factories, farms and railways.
- ☑ In March 1917, after defeating Russia, it seemed as if Germany was poised to defeat the Allies. However, the USA joined in April 1917 and the Allies made a number of important advances.
- ☑ In 1918, Germany wanted to bring a swift end to the war, with the Spring Offensive *(p.84)* from March to July. When this failed, Germany began to consider surrender.

How did the Allies react to the armistice at the end of the First World War?

Britain, France and the USA celebrated the end of the conflict. They were happy the war was over, due to the economic and social impact it had had on them.

What was the reaction to the armistice in Germany at the end of the First World War?

Many Germans were upset at how the war had ended. German soldiers believed the armistice would not last and fighting would resume again; they couldn't believe that they had lost.

What was the difference between the armistice and the Treaty of Versailles at the end of the First World War?

The armistice at the end of the war was different from the Treaty of Versailles, as it was a temporary measure until an official peace settlement could be agreed.

DID YOU KNOW?

The armistice was signed in a railway carriage in Compiegne, France. Hitler used the same railway carriage to accept the French surrender in 1940.

Quizzes, amazing exam preparation tools and more at GCSEHistory.com

HAD GERMANY BEEN DEFEATED?

Armistice and defeat.

 Was Germany defeated in the First World War?

Germany requested an armistice, and this was signed between Germany and the Allies on 11th November 1918. This was the formal end to the fighting while a peace treaty was negotiated.

 What were the reasons for the German defeat in the First World War?

There were a number of reasons for Germany's overall defeat in the First World War:

- ☑ Food and famine. Germany's agricultural production was poor and it relied on foreign imports. However, the British naval blockade starved Germany of these, and there was a series of bad harvests. As the Germans starved, they rioted against the government.

- ☑ Political turmoil. There was a series of riots and revolts against the government. In October there was a naval mutiny, followed by revolutions in Munich and, finally, riots in Berlin. This caused the kaiser to abdicate.

- ☑ Military defeat. Germany realised it was facing a military defeat. With the failure of the Ludendorff Offensive *(p. 84)*, the introduction of two million US troops and its allies surrendering, Germany knew it could no longer continue the fight.

DID YOU KNOW?

The armistice on the Western Front officially began at 11:00am on the 11th of November 1918.

OUTCOMES OF THE FIRST WORLD WAR

By 1919, it was called The Great War for Civilization.

 What were the outcomes of the First World War?

The First World War had a massive impact on all the nations involved in terms of damage, expenditure and lives.

 What was the impact of the First World War on Britain?

Britain suffered heavily as a result of the First World War.

- ☑ Nearly one million British and empire soldiers were killed in the conflict.
- ☑ About 100,000 British civilians died.
- ☑ There were approximately 1.7 million British people injured.

 What was the impact of the First World War on France?

Although France was victorious in the First World War, along with the other Allies, the country was vastly affected by the impact of the war and the damage it caused.

- ☑ There were approximately 1.4 million French military deaths.
- ☑ About 300,000 French civilians were killed.
- ☑ About 4.3 million French citizens were wounded.

What was the impact of the First World War on Russia?

Russia was badly affected by the First World War and had surrendered to Germany before the end.

- ☑ Approximately 1.8 million Russian soldiers were killed.
- ☑ About 500,000 Russian civilians died.
- ☑ Roughly 4 million Russian soldiers were wounded.
- ☑ Russia signed the Treaty of Brest-Litovsk *(p.71)* in March 1918, which surrendered around 25% of Russian land to Germany.

What was the impact of the First World War on Germany?

As a defeated nation, Germany was at the mercy of the victors of the war. However, it had already suffered heavily in the fighting.

- ☑ About 2 million German soldiers were killed.
- ☑ About 4.2 million German soldiers were wounded.
- ☑ Although few German civilians were directly killed by the fighting, there were around half a million deaths from malnutrition and disease.
- ☑ The Allied blockade of Germany caused serious food shortages in Germany until July 1919.

What was the impact of the First World War on the USA?

The USA suffered less heavily than other countries in the First World War but still sustained casualties.

- ☑ Around 100,000 American soldiers died in the conflict.
- ☑ There were about 757 American civilian deaths.
- ☑ About 200,000 Americans were wounded.

What was the impact of the First World War on Italy?

Italy also suffered losses during the First World War.

- ☑ Italy lost approximately 500,000 soldiers in the fighting.
- ☑ About 3,400 Italian civilians were killed.
- ☑ Nearly a million Italian soldiers were wounded.

What was the impact of the First World War on the Ottoman Empire?

The Ottoman Empire collapsed as a result of the war. There were 4 key outcomes:

- ☑ The Sultan was forced to sign the Treaty of Sevres in 1920.
- ☑ The Ottoman Empire was broken up and some land along the Turkish coast was given to Greece.
- ☑ Nationalist forces led by Mustapha Kemal rose up against Greek occupation and began a war to regain their lost territory.
- ☑ France and Britain withdrew their troops and the Greeks were defeated. The new state of Turkey was able to negotiate a better treaty signed at Lausanne in 1923.

> ### DID YOU KNOW?
>
> People at the time did not call the war, the 'First World War'. That has been applied in more modern times. By 1919 it was called The Great War for Civilization, or simply, The Great War.

Quizzes, amazing exam preparation tools and more at GCSEHistory.com

FIELD MARSHAL DOUGLAS HAIG

'The Butcher of the Somme?'

Who was General Haig?

General Haig was the British commander on the Western Front from December 1915. He is a controversial figure as some titled him 'Butcher of the Somme *(p.45)*', while others believe he was a key factor in winning the war.

What successes did General Haig have?

General Haig had numerous successes during the First World War:

- Haig relieved the pressure on French forces at Verdun *(p.44)* by starting the Somme *(p.45)* Offensive.
- The Battle of Passchendaele *(p.46)* succeeded in weakening the German forces.
- Haig drew German forces away from the Nivelle offensive by leading the Battle of Arras.
- He masterminded victories at Messines in June 1917.
- He was willing to be flexible and experiment with the use of tanks, which had success at Cambrai in 1917.
- He was appointed to win the war for the British, which he ultimately did.

What failures did General Haig have?

Haig had a number of failures during the First World War:

- His tactic of attrition resulted in a huge number of casualties, especially at the battles of the Somme *(p.45)* and Passchendaele *(p.46)* .
- He had a very traditional approach to war, as he was trained as a cavalryman. As such, he was slow to experiment with new methods.
- By 1917, there was still a stalemate. Haig hadn't masterminded an overall victory despite the huge losses.

DID YOU KNOW?

It was not only regular soldiers at risk during the war. For example, over 200 British generals were killed, wounded or taken prisoner by the enemy.

FIELD MARSHALL FOCH

The Supreme Allied Commander.

Who was Marshal Ferdinand Foch?

Ferdinand Foch was a French general, prior to and during the First World War. He was promoted to marshall in the summer of 1918.

What was the role of Marshal Ferdinand Foch?

Foch helped stop the German advance at the Battle of the Marne *(p.31)* in 1914. During the Ludendorff Offensive *(p.84)* of spring 1918, he became commander-in-chief of all Allied armies on the Western Front, known as the 'unified command structure'.

What was Marshall Ferdinand Foch's contribution to victory?

Foch planned the Allied 100 Days counter-offensive in 1918 using the latest tactics and technology. In a coordinated attack, the British attacked in the north at the same time as the French and Americans attacked in the south.

DID YOU KNOW?

Marshall Foch was the commanding general who stopped the last German offensive of the war at the Second Battle of the Marne in July 1918.

GENERAL LAVR KORNILOV

General Kornilov was an experienced officer who fought in the Russo-Japanese War, the First World War and the Russian Civil War.

Who was General Kornilov?

General Lavr Kornilov was a capable Russian general who served under the tsar and the Provisional Government *(p.61)* during the First World War.

When was General Kornilov appointed to his role?

General Kornilov was appointed as commander-in-chief of Russian forces by the Provisional Government *(p.61)* in July 1917.

Why was General Kornilov appointed?

General Kornilov was appointed commander-in-chief to improve army discipline so Russia could win the First World War.

What was the role of General Kornilov?

General Kornilov had 3 main roles in the First World War:

- ☑ He was ruthless and opposed the Petrograd Soviet *(p.66)* and left-wing groups.
- ☑ He was suspected of trying to overthrow the Provisional Government *(p.61)* in July 1917 after he was ordered to bring troops to Petrograd to deal with the July uprising. This was known as the Kornilov affair.
- ☑ General Kornilov was sacked and the Provisional Government *(p.61)* lost the support of the army.

What were the results of General Kornilov's actions?

There were 2 main results of General Kornilov's actions in the Kornilov Affair:

- ☑ The Provisional Government *(p.61)* gave weapons to the Petrograd Soviet *(p.66)* to arm the Bolsheviks to defend Petrograd against General Kornilov.
- ☑ He was arrested on 1st September, 1917.

How did General Kornilov die?

General Kornilov escaped and fought with the Whites during the civil war, in which he died.

FIELD MARSHAL SIR JOHN FRENCH

The first commander of the BEF.

Who was Field Marshal Sir John French?

Field Marshal Sir John French was one the key British commanders on the Western Front during the First World War.

What did Field Marshal Sir John French do?

Field Marshal Sir John French had several roles during the war:

- ☑ He was the first commanding officer of the British Expeditionary Force *(p.29)*. He led them to France in 1914.
- ☑ He was replaced in December 1915 because he had lost the trust of the British prime minister, David Lloyd George.
- ☑ From 1916-1918, he was sent to Britain to command the British Home Forces stationed in Britain.

GENERAL ALEKSEI BRUSILOV

A highly competent tsarist officer, who later joined the Bolshevik Red Army.

Who was General Brusilov?

General Brusilov was a Russian, considered one of the best generals to have fought in the First World War.

What did General Brusilov do?

General Brusilov commanded several Russian armies and fought at the Battle of Tannenberg *(p.57)*, where he showed great skill as a commander.

What was General Brusilov known as?

He was known as 'The Iron General' for his aggressive leadership.

What was the significance of General Brusilov?

General Brusilov was a highly respected commander and was significant for 4 reasons:

☑ He led the main Russian attack on the Eastern Front in 1916. The Brusilov Offensive *(p.58)* came very close to knocking the Austro-Hungarian forces out the of the war.

☑ He created highly successful tactics for assaulting trenches. The Germans copied his tactics and used them in the Ludendorff Offensive *(p.84)* of 1918.

☑ Despite the success of the Brusilov Offensive *(p.58)* his brutal attacks left so many Russians dead that it helped to lead to the collapse of the Russian Army in 1917.

☑ He joined the Bolsheviks in 1918 and led the Red Army cavalry during the Russian Civil War *(p.73)*.

DID YOU KNOW?

General Aleksei Brusilov is considered by some historians to be one of the greatest generals of the First World War. Events on the Eastern Front are often overlooked in favour of the Western Front.

GENERAL ERICH LUDENDORFF

A hero of the Eastern Front and commander of Germany's last gamble on the Western Front.

 Who was General von Ludendorff?

General von Ludendorff was considered one of Germany's greatest generals of the First World War. He was seen as a hero for his efforts on both the Eastern and Western Fronts. He became involved with the Nazi Party's failed Munich Beer Hall Putsch in 1923.

 When was General Ludendorff important?

General von Ludendorff was important between the years 1914 and 1923.

 What was the role of General Ludendorff in the First World War?

General Ludendorff had 4 key roles during the war:

☑ General Ludendorff was the second in command to Field Marshal Hindenburg *(p.95)*. Together they commanded the German armies on the Eastern Front from 1914 to 1916.

☑ General Ludendorff helped to defeat the Russians at Tannenberg *(p.57)* in 1914.

☑ From August 1916 until October 1918, General Ludendorff became the most powerful *(p.16)* man in Germany, leading a military dictatorship for the Kaiser.

☑ General Ludendorff commanded the final German offensive of the war in 1918.

 What was the significance of General Ludendorff during the First World War?

General Ludendorff was significant in the First World War for 4 key reasons:

☑ His victory at Tannenberg *(p.57)* saved Germany from defeat.

☑ He refused to accept offers of peace negotiations from the United States and prolonged the war as much as possible.

☑ He supported unrestricted submarine warfare *(p.49)* even though he was warned it could force America to declare war on Germany.

☑ He created the 'stab-in-the-back' myth to cover for his own failings and place the blame on democratic politicians who led the German Republic after the war.

Why was General von Ludendorff important to the Weimar Republic?

General von Ludendorff was important during the Weimar Republic for 5 main reasons:

- ☑ He led the massive German offensive against the Allies in March 1918 called the 'Ludendorff Offensive *(p.84)*' which failed.
- ☑ He created the stab-in-the-back myth to cover for his own failings during the war and place the blame on democratic politicians who led the Weimar Republic after the war.
- ☑ He supported Dr Wolfgang Kapp in the Kapp Putsch in March 1920.
- ☑ He took part in the Nazi Party's failed Beer Hall Putsch in November 1923.
- ☑ He was put on trial because of his role in the Munich Beer Hall Putsch but was found not guilty.

DID YOU KNOW?

In 1904, General Erich Ludendorff was a member of the Germany Army's great general staff where he was heavily involved in the development of the Schlieffen Plan.

FIELD MARSHAL PAUL VON HINDENBURG

He became the supreme commander of all the Central Powers' forces, and defeated Russia.

 Who was Field Marshal Paul von Hindenburg?

Field Marshal Paul von Hindenburg was an important German military figure in the First World War and was elected the second president of the Weimar Republic.

 When was Field Marshal Hindenburg important?

Field Marshal Paul von Hindenburg was important from 1914 to 1934.

 What was role of Field Marshal Hindenburg in the First World War?

Field Marshal Hindenburg had 4 key roles during the First World War:

- ☑ Field Marshal Hindenburg commanded the German armies on the Eastern Front with his friend and second in command, General Ludendorff.
- ☑ By the end of the war, he commanded the entire Imperial German Army and those of the other Central Powers.
- ☑ He ruled Germany as part of a military dictatorship until October 1918.
- ☑ It was Hindenburg who told the kaiser that the German Army would not continue to fight in October 1918.

What was the significance of Field Marshal Hindenburg in the First World War?

Field Marshal Hindenburg was significant for 2 key reasons during the war:

- ☑ He became the hero of Tannenberg *(p.57)*, saving Germany from defeat in 1914.
- ☑ Along with General Ludendorff, it was his policies that would lead Germany to defeat in 1918, especially his support for unrestricted submarine warfare *(p.49)*.

 What was significance of Field Marshal Hindenburg in the Weimar Republic?

Paul von Hindenburg played a significant role in the Weimar Republic for 6 key reasons:

- ☑ He became the commander of the Germany army in 1916 and was in charge when Germany surrendered in November 1918. He allowed General von Ludendorff to take the blame for the defeat.
- ☑ He was elected president of the Weimar Republic in April 1925.
- ☑ Hitler opposed him in the presidential elections in March and April 1932 and lost.
- ☑ Hindenburg is best known for attempting to block Hitler from becoming the chancellor of Weimar Germany.
- ☑ However, he was persuaded by Franz von Papen to appoint Hitler as chancellor on 30th January, 1933 and thus aided the collapse of the Weimar Republic.
- ☑ His death in 1934 was a key event in Hitler's creation of a dictatorship as Hitler merged the role of chancellor and president into one: the Führer.

 ### When did Paul von Hindenburg die?

President Paul von Hindenburg died on 2nd August, 1934.

DID YOU KNOW?

Paul von Hindenburg was a German war hero. The Nazis named a series of zeppelins after him during the 1930s, which were the largest passenger zepplins of their time. In 1937, the LZ 129 Hindenburg caught fire, and 35 passengers and crew out of the 97 people on board died.

ADMIRAL JOHN JELLICOE

'...the best officer the Navy has ever had since Nelson.' - Winston Churchill on Admiral Jellicoe, 1912.

 ### Who was Admiral Jellicoe?

Admiral Jellicoe was one of Britain's most senior naval officers.

 ### What did Admiral Jellicoe do?

Admiral Jellicoe was the most important British naval commander during the First World War:

- ☑ He was the commander of the British Grand Fleet that defended Britain from the German High Seas Fleet.
- ☑ He commanded the British Grand Fleet at the Battle of Jutland *(p.49)* in May 1916.
- ☑ Admiral Jellicoe was sacked in 1917 for disagreeing with the tactic of using convoys to combat the threat of U-boats.

 ### What was the significance of Admiral Jellicoe?

Admiral Jellicoe was significant for 2 reasons:

- ☑ He forced the German High Seas Fleet to remain in harbour during the war.
- ☑ Winston Churchill said that Admiral Jellicoe was 'the only man on either side who could lose the war in an afternoon' - meaning that to lose the Battle of Jutland *(p.49)* would mean a British defeat in the war.

DID YOU KNOW?

John Rushworth Jellicoe was born in Southampton. He joined the Royal Navy in 1872 and served in the Egyptian War of 1882, and continued to distinguish himelf in the years prior to the First World War.

A

Abdicate - to give up a position of power or a responsibility.

Abolish, Abolished - to stop something, or get rid of it.

Abolition - the act of abolishing something, i.e. to stop or get rid of it.

Agricultural - relating to agriculture.

Agriculture - an umbrella term to do with farming, growing crops or raising animals.

Alliance - a union between groups or countries that benefits each member.

Allies - parties working together for a common objective, such as countries involved in a war. In both world wars, 'Allies' refers to those countries on the side of Great Britain.

Ambassador - someone, often a diplomat, who represents their state, country or organisation in a different setting or place.

Ammunition - collective term given to bullets and shells.

Amputate, Amputation - to surgically remove a limb from someone's body.

Archaic - to be very old or old-fashioned.

Aristocrat - a person who belongs to the aristocracy.

Armistice - an agreement between two or more opposing sides in a war to stop fighting.

Artillery - large guns used in warfare.

Assassinate - to murder someone, usually an important figure, often for religious or political reasons.

Assassination - the act of murdering someone, usually an important person.

Attrition - the act of wearing down an enemy until they collapse through continued attacks.

Autocracy - a system of government where the ruler has absolute power over their country.

Autocrat - a ruler who has absolute power over their country.

B

Bankrupt - to be insolvent; to have run out of resources with which to pay existing debts.

Blockade - a way of blocking or sealing an area to prevent goods, supplies or people from entering or leaving. It often refers to blocking transport routes.

Bolshevik, Bolsheviks - was a Russian radical Marxist revolutionary group, founded by Vladimir Lenin and Alexander Bogdanov in 1903. A Bolshevik is someone who is a member of that party.

Bourgeoisie - the capitalists who owned the means of production, i.e. land, banks and factories, in Marxist ideology.

Box barrage - The firing shells at the enemy on three sides to prevent them retreating or sending reinforcements into a battle.

C

Campaign - a political movement to get something changed; in military terms, it refers to a series of operations to achieve a goal.

Casualties - people who have been injured or killed, such as during a war, accident or catastrophe.

Cavalry - the name given to soldiers who fight on horseback.

Ceasefire - when the various sides involved in conflict agree to stop fighting.

Censorship - the control of information in the media by a government, whereby information considered obscene or unacceptable is suppressed.

Chancellor - a senior state official who, in some countries, is the head of the government and responsible for the day-to-day running of the nation.

Civil rights - the rights a citizen has to political or social freedoms, such as the right to vote or freedom of speech.

Civilian - a non-military person.

Claim - someone's assertion of their right to something - for example, a claim to the throne.

Coalition, Coalitions - a temporary alliance, such as when a group of countries fights together.

Colonies, Colony - a country or area controlled by another country and occupied by settlers.

Communism - the belief, based on the ideas of Karl Marx, that all people should be equal in society without government, money or private property. Everything is owned by by the people, and each person receives according to need.

Communist - a believer in communism.

Conscription - mandatory enlistment of people into a state service, usually the military.

Consolidate - to strengthen a position, often politically, by bringing several things together into a more effective whole.

Constitution - rules, laws or principles that set out how a country is governed.

Constitutional monarchy - political system in which a monarch's powers and authority are limited by a constitution.

Convoy - a group of ships or vehicles travelling together, usually protected by armed troops.

Corrupt - when someone is willing to act dishonestly for their own personal gain.

Council - an advisory or administrative body set up to manage the affairs of a place or organisation. The Council of the League of Nations contained the organisation's most powerful members.

Counter-attack - an attack made in response to one by an opponent.

Coup - a sudden, violent and illegal overthrow of the government by a small group - for example, the chiefs of an army.

Creeping barrage - a slowly advancing artillery bombardment which attacking troops can follow for protection.

Culture - the ideas, customs, and social behaviour of a particular people or society.

D

Deadlock - a situation where no action can be taken and neither side can make progress against the other; effectively a draw.

Debt - when something, usually money, is owed by a person, organisation or institution to another.

Decree - an official order with the force of law behind it.

Democracy - a political system where a population votes for its government on a regular basis. The word is Greek for 'the rule of people' or 'people power'.

Democratic - relating to or supporting the principles of democracy.

Deportation - the act of deporting someone.

Deterrent - something that discourages an action or behaviour.

Dictatorship - a form of government where an individual or small group has total power, ruling without tolerance for other views or opposition.

Dud - a bomb, shell or mine that fails to explode.

E

Economic - relating to the economy; also used when justifying something in terms of profitability.

Economy - a country, state or region's position in terms of production and consumption of goods and services, and the supply of money.

Empire - a group of states or countries ruled over and controlled by a single monarch.

Encircle, Encirclement - a military term for enemy forces isolating and surrounding their target.

Extreme - furthest from the centre or any given point. If someone holds extreme views, they are not moderate and are considered radical.

F

Famine - a severe food shortage resulting in starvation and death, usually the result of bad harvests.

Fasting - to deliberately refrain from eating, and often drinking, for a period of time.

Federal - in US politics this means 'national', referring to the whole country rather than any individual state.

Foreign policy - a government's strategy for dealing with other nations.

Front - in war, the area where fighting is taking place.

Frontier - a line or border between two areas.

G

Gangrene - the death of body tissue due to either lack of blood or serious bacterial infection.

H

Harvest - the process of gathering and collecting crops.

Heir - someone who is entitled to property or rank following the current owner or holder's death.

Home front - a term covering the activities of civilians while their nation is at war, including the effect it has on their everyday lives.

I

Idealist - someone who believes in idealism and works towards the perfect world.

Illiterate - unable to read or write.

Immigrant - someone who moves to another country.

Immigration - the act of coming to a foreign country with the intention of living there permanently.

Imperial, Imperialisation, Imperialism, Imperialist - is the practice or policy of taking possession of, and extending political and economic control over other areas or territories. Imperialism always requires the use of military, political or economic power by a stronger nation over that of a weaker one. An imperialist is someone who supports or practices imperialism and imperial relates to a system of empire, for example the British Empire.

Import - to bring goods or services into a different country to sell.

Independence, Independent - to be free of control, often meaning by another country, allowing the people of a nation the ability to govern themselves.

Industrial - related to industry, manufacturing and/or production.

Industrialisation, Industrialise, Industrialised - the process of developing industry in a country or region where previously there was little or none.

Industry - the part of the economy concerned with turning raw materials into into manufactured goods, for example making furniture from wood.

Infantry - soldiers who march and fight on foot.

Inflation - the general increase in the prices of goods which means money does not buy as much as it used to.

Infrastructure - the basic physical and organisational facilities a society or country needs to function, such as transport networks, communications and power.

Interim - in the meantime; during an intervening period.

International relations - the relationships between different countries.

K

Kaiser - the German word for a king or emperor.

L

Left wing - used to describe political groups or individuals with beliefs that are usually centered around socialism and the idea of reform.

Legitimacy, Legitimate - accepted by law or conforming to the rules; can be defended as valid.

Liberal - politically, someone who believes in allowing personal freedom without too much control by the government or state.

Limb - an arm or leg.

Lord, Lords - a man of high status, wealth and authority.

M

Malnutrition - lack of proper nutrition caused by not eating enough of the right things or not having enough to eat. It can also be caused by the body not being able to use the food that is eaten.

Mass - an act of worship in the Catholic Church.

Massacre - the deliberate and brutal slaughter of many people.

Medic - someone who has medical knowledge but is not a doctor.

Merchant ships - unarmed ships used for carrying supplies and goods.

Merchant, Merchants - someone who sells goods or services.

Middle class - refers to the socio-economic group which includes people who are educated and have professional jobs, such as teachers or lawyers.

Military force - the use of armed forces.

Mine - an explosive device usually hidden underground or underwater.

Minister - a senior member of government, usually responsible for a particular area such as education or finance.

Mobilisation - the action of a country getting ready for war by preparing and organising its armed forces.

Monarchists - people in favour of living in a country governed by a monarchy.

Monarchy - a form of government in which the head of state is a monarch, a king or queen.

Morale - general mood of a group of people.

Morass - an area of swampy or very wet and muddy ground which is difficult to cross.

Mutiny - a rebellion or revolt, in particular by soldiers or sailors against their commanding officers.

N

Nationalism, Nationalist, Nationalistic - identifying with your own nation and supporting its interests, often to the detriment or exclusion of other nations.

No man's land - the land between the opposing sides' trenches in the First World War.

O

Occupation - the action, state or period when somewhere is taken over and occupied by a military force.

Offensive - another way of saying an attack or campaign.

P

POW, Prisoner of war, Prisoners of war - somebody who has been captured and taken prisoner by enemy forces.

Parliament - a group of politicians who make the laws of their country, usually elected by the population.

Patriotic - a strong love of and support for one's country.

Peasant - a poor farmer.

Plague - a contagious disease that spreads rapidly.

Population - the number of people who live in a specified place.

Poverty - the state of being extremely poor.

Prejudice - prejudgement - when you assume something about someone based on a feature like their religion or skin colour, rather than knowing it as fact.

President - the elected head of state of a republic.

Prevent, Preventative, Preventive - steps taken to stop something from happening.

Production - a term used to describe how much of something is made, for example saying a factory has a high production rate.

Propaganda - biased information aimed at persuading people to think a certain way.

Province, Provinces - part of an empire or a country denoting areas that have been divided for administrative purposes.

Psychological - referring to a person's mental or emotional state.

Q

Quagmire - an area of swampy or very wet and muddy ground which is difficult to cross.

R

Radical, Radicalism - people who want complete or extensive change, usually politically or socially.

Raid - a quick surprise attack on the enemy.

Rationing - limiting goods that are in high demand and short supply.

Rebels - people who rise in opposition or armed resistance against an established government or leader.

Reconnaissance - observation of an enemy in order to gain useful information such as its position, strategy or capabilities.

Regent - the person who rules when the king is away, incapacitated or too young to rule.

Reparations - payments made by the defeated countries in a war to the victors to help pay for the cost of and damage from the fighting.

Republic - a state or country run by elected representatives and an elected/nominated president. There is no monarch.

Requisition - to take something, usually by official order, such as a government taking food from peasants.

Revolution - the forced overthrow of a government or social system by its own people.

Right wing - a political view with beliefs centred around nationalism and a desire for an authoritarian government opposed to communism.

Riots - violent disturbances involving a crowd of people.

Rolling barrage - a slowly advancing artillery bombardment which attacking troops can follow for protection.

S

Salient - in military terms, a piece of land that protrudes into enemy territory; also known as a bulge.

Slavic people, Slavs - the main ethnic group of people living in Eastern Europe.

Socialism - a political and economic system where most resources, such as factories and businesses, are owned by the state or workers with the aim of achieving greater equality between rich and poor.

Socialist - one who believes in the principles of socialism.

Soviet - an elected workers' council at local, regional or national level in the former Soviet Union. It can also be a reference to the Soviet Union or the USSR.

Splendid isolation - a British foreign policy in the 19th century which aimed to focus on the British Empire and keep Britain out of European wars.

Stalemate - a situation where no action can be taken and neither side can make progress against the other; effectively a draw.

State, States - an area of land or a territory ruled by one government.

Strategy - a plan of action outlining how a goal will be achieved.

Strike - a refusal by employees to work as a form of protest, usually to bring about change in their working conditions. It puts pressure on their employer, who cannot run the business without workers.

Symptom - an indication of something, such as a sign of a particular illness.

T

Tactic - a strategy or method of achieving a goal.

Territories, Territory - an area of land under the control of a ruler/ country.

The crown, The throne - phrases used to represent royal power. For example, if someone 'seizes the throne' it means they have taken control. Can also refer to physical objects.

Treaty - a formal agreement, signed and ratified by two or more parties.

Tsar - the Russian word for emperor; can also be spelled 'czar'.

U

U-boat - the German name for a submarine.

Ultimatum - a final demand, with the threat of consequences if it is not met.

Upper class - a socio-economic group consisting of the richest people in society who are wealthy because they own land or property.

W

Weltpolitik - Germany's pre-First World War foreign policy which aimed to turn Germany into a global power by acquiring overseas colonies and developing its navy.

Working class - socio-economic group consisting of those engaged in waged labour, especially manual work or industry, who typically do not have much money.